You Are What You Say

Cure for the
Troublesome
Tongue

You Are What You Say

Cure for the Troublesome Tongue

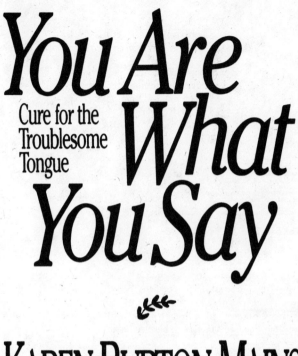

KAREN BURTON MAINS

Zondervan Books
Zondervan Publishing House
Grand Rapids, Michigan

YOU ARE WHAT YOU SAY
Copyright © 1988 by Karen Burton Mains

Zondervan Books are published by
Zondervan Publishing House
1415 Lake Drive, S.E.
Grand Rapids, MI 49506

Library of Congress Cataloging in Publication Data

Mains, Karen Burton.
You are what you say.

1. Conversation. 2. Words, Obscene. 3. Truthfulness and falsehood.
4. Christian life—1960–
I. Title.
BJ2121.M32   1988   177'.2   885687
ISBN 0-310-34211-2

Unless otherwise indicated, Scripture references are taken
from the Revised Standard Version, copyright © 1946, 1952, 1971,
by the Division of Christian Education of the National Council
of the Churches of Christ in the United States of America.
Used by permission.

The following publishers have generously given permission to use extended
quotations from copyrighted works: From *Key to a Loving Heart*, by Karen
Mains. Reprinted by permission of David C. Cook Publishing Company. From
Collected Poems, by Edna St. Vincent Millay. Copyright 1917, 1928, 1945,
1955 by Edna St. Vincent Millay and Norma Millay Ellis. Reprinted by
permission of the estate of Norma Millay Ellis. From *Eighty Fairy Tales*, by
Hans Christian Andersen, translated by R. P. Keigwin. Translation copyright
© 1976 by Skandinavisk Bogforlag Flensteds Forlag. Reprinted by permission
of Pantheon Books, a Division of Random House, Inc. From *Canticle of the
Bride*, by John Michael Talbot. Copyright 1980 by Birdwing Music/Cherry
Lane Music Publishing Company, Inc. Reprinted by permission of The
Sparrow Corporation.

Printed in the United States of America

88 89 90 91 92 / LP / 10 9 8 7 6 5 4 3 2

CONTENTS

TONGUE: *A tongue that is dry, dark and furred indicates an unhealthful condition. A tongue that is moist and clean is of the normal appearance. The healthy tongue can be moved quickly or slowly in all directions. In people who have over-activity of the thyroid gland, the tongue moves quickly. Those who have underactivity of the thyroid, have a sluggish tongue. People who are weak or exhausted and those in a stupor or coma cannot project the tongue far. Sometimes a nervous condition causes the tongue to tremble. Paralysis may affect one side of the tongue only, so that the healthy side will push the tongue toward the paralyzed side. People may suffer with a burning of the tongue, which seems in many instances to be a psychosomatic condition. Burning of the tongue occurs in pellagra and in various vitamin deficiencies. Elevations of the papillae of the tongue develop in a condition called geographic tongue. In pernicious anemia, the tongue assumes a most unhealthful appearance, which is overcome by taking vitamin B12.*

Morris Fishbein
The Handy Home Medical Adviser

PREFACE
Words Have Power

As a child, whenever I wished aloud for someone's death, my mother, ever the romantic moralist, told me a story out of the days of her early marriage. She and my father had lived in the lower part of a two-flat apartment. The young woman upstairs was frustrated and often angry about a colicky baby. One day, in a passion she complained, "I hate that child! I wish he would die!"

Very soon after this outburst, the infant did die—a crib death; and when the bereaved woman next saw my mother she sobbed, "I didn't mean what I said. I didn't mean it—I didn't want my baby to die."

Mother's point was that I should never say I hated anyone, that I should never wish anyone's death. The possibility was all too real that something tragic might occur to the hated person. Death had a way of sneaking in; then we would be left to deal with the guilt and grief from our own words.

But as a child I wove richer fabric from my mother's tale (and

I heard the story frequently because I was inclined to pronounce curses upon the heads of friends who disenchanted me; a restrained inclination still, I concluded that words, words in themselves, are powerful.

Dylan Thomas, the Welsh poet, wrote:

> The first poems I knew were nursery rhymes, and before I could read them for myself I had come to love just the words of them; the words alone. What the words stood for, symbolized, or meant, was of very secondary importance. What mattered was the sound of them. . .and these words were, to me, as the notes of bells, the sounds of musical instruments, the noises of wind, sea, and rain, the rattle of milk-carts, the clopping of hooves on cobbles, the finger- ing of branches on a window pane. . .I did not care what the words said, overmuch, nor what happened to Jack and Jill and the Mother Goose rest of them; I cared for the shapes of sound that their names made in my ears; I cared for the colours the words cast on my eyes.

From a purely technical viewpoint, every good writer knows that certain words—and certain sounds in words—evoke emotional responses in the human soul. Gerard Manley Hopkins, a major Victorian poet in England, experienced a spiritual crisis in 1866 that eventually led him to become a Jesuit priest. Read these words slowly; best of all, read them out loud.

> As kingfishers catch fire, dragonflies draw flame;
> As tumbled over rim in roundy wells
> Stones ring; like each tucked string tells, each hung bell's
> Bow swung finds tongue to fling out broad its name.

Rhythm, cadence, repetition, the round sound of O's — somehow the human heart leans, yearning toward this kind of verbal beauty.

In the book *Writing the Natural Way, Using Right-Brain Techniques to Release Your Expressive Power*, the author,

Gabriele Rico, maintains that the right hemisphere of the brain is the seat of design, and repetitive patterns of language evoke a powerful and satisfying response from the right brain:

> Recurring words, sounds, images. . .have the same powerful effect that a recurring melody has in music, recurring foliage in a landscape, recurring colors in a painting; we react to them emotionally. In language, we are more likely to remember recurring patterns—for example, "of the people, by the people, for the people. . ." from the Gettysburg Address—because of their powerful effect on the right brain. For this reason, much persuasive writing, and especially speeches, contain recurrences . . . learning to use recurrences—the *meaningful* repetition of words, images, ideas, phrases, sound, objects or actions throughout a piece of writing empowers it because of the right hemisphere of the brain's response to it.

Beautiful words have become for me a substitute for valium—the antidepressant drug. If people could only learn to take words instead of pills!

A close friend was scheduled to visit our home. This man frequently enriches conversation with memorized quotations, so I thought I would take the time to memorize a poem in his honor. Having chosen Edna St. Vincent Millay's "God's Worlds" (a poem I've always loved and had promised myself I would make my own—some day), I walked through the autumn world of that year, my memory card in hand:

> O world, I cannot hold thee close enough!
>   Thy winds, thy wide grey skies!
>   Thy mists, that roll and rise!
> Thy woods, this autumn day, that ache and sag
> And all but cry with colour! That gaunt crag
> To crush! To lift the lean of that black bluff!
> World, World, I cannot get thee close enough!
>
> Long have I known a glory in it all,
>   But never knew I this:

> Here such a passion is
> As stretcheth me apart,—Lord, I do fear
> Thou'st made the world too beautiful this year;
> My soul is all but out of me,—let fall
> No burning leaf; prithee, let no bird call.

The days of memorization, however, were days particularly filled with stress. I oversaw the logistics of family, five people needing to be in different places all at the same time, chaffeured, comforted, and financed; I encouraged a husband while he recorded twelve broadcasts in the studio for our nationally syndicated fifteen-minute radio daily. I spoke for a day and half at a convention of fifteen hundred youth ministers (a stressful enough event in itself), attended to a personal inner glitch in my own soul that raised sudden surprising demands, changed linens on beds between two sets of houseguests, swiped at the guest bathroom, dealt with the inevitable crises of adolescents, and tried to prepare reasonable facsimilies of decent meals. One of those weeks!

Yet the words of the poet—*that gaunt crag to crush, to lift the lean of that black fluff*—calmed me, gave me a sense of peace. As I repeated the lovely lines over and over—*here such a passion is as stretcheth me apart*—I began to experience how the memorizing of beautiful words can be quieting and restorative. All the mental bats echo-navigating in my mind's belfry, *should do-o-o-o-o's, to do-o-o-o-o's, can't do-o-o-o-o's,* were silenced and replaced by the symmetry and harmony of words.

For me beautiful words are better than valium.

An issue of *Strophes* magazine, the official publication of the National Federation of Poetry Societies, advocated the restorative powers of words by recommending two books that advanced the theory that poetry could be useful as a therapeutic tool. One was a textbook for professionals titled *Poetry Therapy* by Dr. J. J. Leedy of the Cumberland Hospital's Mental Health Clinic in Brooklyn. The second was a book written by Dr.

Smiley Blanton and titled *The Healing Power of Poetry*. The Veteran's Administration, as well, has authorized the use of poetry as a therapy throughout its hospitals and is finding both the writing and reading of poetry an aid to the improved mental condition of patients.

The psalmist knew the power of words ages ago. "This is my comfort in my affliction that thy promise gives me life" (Ps. 119:50). "If thy law had not been my delight, I should have perished in my affliction" (v. 92). "Great peace have those who love thy law; nothing can make them stumble" (v. 165).

One of the reasons people throughout the centuries have loved good and beautiful words, oral story cycles, spoken epic rhymes, words combined into tales, into songs, into poetry is this: There is power in words, even physiological benefit, from knowing and reading great thoughts expressed in great ways.

Marie Avinov was born into the aristocracy of Tsarist Russia, survived the Russian Revolution, the regime of Stalin, and World War II. She writes in her book, *Pilgrimage Through Hell*, about her experience in the Stalinist prison camps. During one transportation, she was marched to a local prison and shoved into a cell made to house thirty but which was now crowded with over a hundred women, prostitutes and aristocrats mixed together. The conditions were unbearable—the prisoners fought with each other over a cube of sugar, over a bit of black bread. One hit another over the head with a bottle. Women were malnourished and sick in the cell, where there was barely room to stand, let alone rest or sit.

It was here that Marie Avinov began to tell the stories she had learned in her own privileged and richly educated past (with inner apologies to the authors for extemporizing parts of plots lost to her memory). The women in the cell became silent, humanized, eager to hear another story, then another. Jules Verne's *Around the World in Eighty Days*, Charlotte Bronte's *Jane Eyre*, Jack London's *The Call of the Wild*, the detective tales of Arthur Conan Doyle—all these soothed beastly responses to inhuman conditions.

When the women became disorderly, the cell block leader would threaten: "If you want to hear more stories, then you must be very quiet. If you don't behave, I'll stop the story telling at once!" Again and again, a chorus of voices rang out with promises to be good. Mrs. Avinov laughingly refers to herself in those terrible days as the Scheherazade of Cell 26.

Words are powerful because they evoke emotional, psychological, spiritual, and intellectual meaning. "Fine writing," says Annie Dillard, the Pulitzer prize-winning author, "with its elaborated imagery and powerful rhythms, has the beauty of both complexity and grandeur. It also has as its distinction a magnificent power to penetrate. . .It is an energy."

John Gardner writes of the power of words in his book *On Moral Fiction:*

> Words conjure emotionally charged images in the reader's mind, and when the words are put together in the proper way, then the proper rhythms—long and short sounds, smooth or ragged, tranquil or rambunctious—we have the queer experience of falling through the print on the page into something like a dream, an imaginary world so real and convincing that when we happen to be jerked out of it by a call from the kitchen or a knock at the door, we stare for an instant in befuddlement at the familiar room where we sat down, half an hour ago, with our book.

And all primitive peoples, with wise childlike intuitions, everywhere suspect what I suspected as a child: that there is power in words, words alone. Consequently, they still give credence to magical chants, to incantations, to sacred verbal formulas, to curses and enchantments. They have much more faith in the power of words than does contemporary man so surfeited with them that he forgets their meaning.

In ancient days, kings, rulers, statesmen, generals, philosophers, and scientists were of necessity poets: it was their sole socially acceptable form of expression. Poetry preceded prose, in the days when writing was unknown to man. The rhythm and meter of poetry provided memorable devices that prose lacked. In the beginning, lyric cries, folk wisdom, tales of tribal heroes, formal odes of jubilation or lamentation, religious teachings, philosophies, pseudosciences, histories of men, men-gods, gods and peoples developed first in the form of poetry; and thus, the common man felt their power.

People today should learn to have more faith in the power of words than they do.

A friend and I meet regularly for lunch. Her marriage has been rocky, and she has become attracted to a man at work who returns her interest. There has been no physical sexuality in their relationship but a great deal of verbal sexuality. "They're just words," she said to me, reporting one of their mutual exchanges. "This isn't sinning. Words aren't actions."

I had to tell her that I believed words are actions; some words are so powerful they undo worlds, they create havoc, they destroy well-ordered societies, they bring the downfall of dynasties, kingdoms, and clans, they speak murder, they rip truth apart—they shatter marriages with spoken adultery.

Later my friend realized that the words of mutual sexual attraction were winding a tight emotional and psychological bondage by means of these prolonged discussions, these sexual incantations. "Words are actions," she said to me later.

The sing-song chant is utterly in error. "Sticks and stones may break your bones, but words will never harm you." Never teach this to children. They need to know that they may heal sooner from physical wounds than verbal ones. How is it that something said to me years ago still has the power to evoke embarrassment or anguish (and I scarcely remember the fall that carved my knee with a scar and recall the pain not at all)? How is it that someone recollects the casual, caustic remark I jettisoned into a conversation (though I have long forgotten the incident) and now reckons with the grief they have carried from my thoughtless verbal action (of which I had no intent)?

No, words have power. There is no such things as "just words."

Christ understood the profound power of words. "Peace! Be still!" he spoke to the wild wind and waves. The raging sea was calmed. Try this. Stand out in the next thunderstorm and say, "Be quiet!" At that moment of abject futility, one begins to consider the authority Christ invested in words. "Be thou healed," speaks Christ and skin cells bond, leaching blood clots, optic fibers transmit, muscles and ligaments cohere, tissue flowers into whole flesh, the fillament drum vibrates with ear-sound.

Proverbs 18:21 says, "Death and life are in the power of the tongue," and we must learn to believe this if we are to use words again in godlike fashion.

Emily Dickinson was aware of the power of words to wound:

> She dealt her pretty words like Blades
> How glittering they shown
> And every One unbared a Nerve
> Or wantoned with a Bone.

She also believed that words, greatly conceived and expressed, were sacramental in their efficacy. A sacrament, according to the dictionary, is anything that conveys something of God in it. Certain words said in certain ways can be the very tongue of God to the listener.

When the apostle John chose a noun to describe Christ, he chose the *Word*. The prologue to John's gospel resounds, "In the beginning was the Word, and the Word was with God, and the Word was God. . .in him was life. . .and the Word became flesh and dwelt among us" (1:1, 4, 14). Christ is the Word that is life that became flesh.

We may never attain to Christ's verbal authority, but we learn to speak his words in our restless chaotic world; and when we speak life to the world, the Word becomes the word of our very mouths. This incarnational reality is profound and to me, a wordsmith striking the anvil of heart and mind, extremely exciting. I can speak sacramentally, actually mouth Christ to the world; he can literally speak life through me.

But first I must really believe that my words can speak life or death, that they are not "just words"; I must take the teachings of Proverbs to heart: ". . .the babbling of a fool brings ruin near. . .with his mouth the godless man would destroy his neighbor. . .by the blessing of the upright a city is exalted, but it is overthrown by the mouth of the wicked. . .a gentle tongue is a tree of life, but perverseness in it breaks the spirit" (10:14; 11:9, 11; 15:4).

And once I have become convinced that this organ, the tongue, is riddled with mouth disease, that it speaks illness instead of health into the world around me, I need to submit to intensive examination, determine the proper diagnosis, and then seek a cure. I want to tame this unruly member, small in size but mighty in potential, lest it cause anguish, lest it break spirits, lest it bring my cherished work to ruin, lest it deal death to the new life of one I love, frail in its beginning.

I must learn to hunger after word health; I must learn to appropriate my tongue's power in holy ways.

The Diagnosis

When the great Rabbi Gamaliel, one of the wisest, told his servants: "Bring me something good," the servants brought a tongue. The Rabbi said: "Go to the market, bring me something bad." Again, the servant brought a tongue, saying: "A tongue, my master, may be the source of either good or evil. If it is good, there is nothing better. If it is bad, there is nothing worse."

Talmud

1

THE EXAMINATION
Stick Out Your Tongue

Stick out your tongue; say ah-h-h-h-h."

How many times since childhood have we heard these instructions? Stick out your tongue; say ah-h-h-h-h.

In the Mains's family household, one child took those words as a personal challenge. "If anyone puts a stick down my throat, I'll vomit," he invariably warned me each time we headed toward a pediatrician's office.

"But Joel," I would explain (again). "The doctor has to check your throat. You've been running a temp and complaining about pain when you swallow."

Soon we'd find ourselves in a little cubicle in the doctor's office. Joel would scoot defiantly onto the examining table, his legs swinging rhythmically, his gym shoes thumping against the side. We would wait in the medicinal atmosphere, making mother/son chitchat until the doctor's nurse entered, crisp in white, smiling a most charming smile, one that had calmed and disarmed hundreds of apprehensive children. "What seems to be the matter here?"

When we reported an elevated temperature and trouble with swallowing, she would turn to the jar on the counter that held compressors, those slightly overgrown popsicle sticks.

"I throw up if you put those things down my mouth," Joel invariably warned.

"No," the nurse would reply smoothly, professionally, confidently. "It will only take a moment. Now stick out your tongue. Say ah-h-h-h-h."

With a look of resignation, Joel would stick out his tongue, obediently say, "ah-h-h-h-h"; in would go the compressor; I would close my eyes. Sure enough, gagging and retching.

"He seems to have an oversensitive vomit reactor," I would explain, torn between vaulting parental peevishness and intense loyalty. And as we quickly cleaned up the mess I would ask, "Did you get a look down his throat?"

For a while I regarded Joe's behavior as a major embarrassment. I had failed somewhere as a mother. Wrongly, or rightly, stoicism was the family rule when visiting pediatricians. "Mains's kids don't cry," I would insist in my most practiced positive tone, and sure enough they marched through doctor's offices and family clinics and emergency rooms with the stiff upper lips of Trojan warriors. One of the children endured twelve stitches for a cut above the eye without so much as a whimper. Mains's kids—they were all terrific, proud of their own rigor as they bragged ritualistically at evening meals after medical appointments. Mains's kids don't cry—except Joel.

He not only cried; he also kicked and screamed and hollered. I endured vast waves of emotional trauma while watching my child, a Mains's kid, being forcibly restrained for injections; and, furthermore, none of my parental wiles worked—not promises of a stop at Peterson's Ice Cream Parlor if he controlled himself or overt, bald-faced sibling comparisons such as your older brother and sister have never acted this way and even the baby doesn't cry the way you cry.

Joel just didn't care; and in this matter, his will was stronger than all the five of the rest of us combined. Appealing to his pride was worthless. He punched the self-esteem eject button whenever he entered a pediatrician's waiting room. And time after time, I knew the moment I heard the nurse tell him to stick out his tongue and say ah-h-h-h-h that I was going to be mortified.

I have a feeling that there are a lot of people who are just like Joel was (it is a relief to report that we have turned a behavioral corner). They have an instant, negative reaction whenever anyone says, "Stick out your tongue. Say ah-h-h-h-h."

Just as it was important for a medical professional to examine Joel's tongue for abnormalities that were symptomatic of disease, so your tongue, my tongue, everybody's tongue is an absolute indicator of what kind of disorder may be lodged in our souls and needs to undergo rigorous self-examination.

The truth is: We are literally what we say, even when we think we have fooled people by our carefully chosen words. In the end our tongues always betray symptoms of soul sickness. Proverbs says, "For the lips of a loose woman drip honey, and her speech is smoother than oil; but in the end she is bitter as wormwood, sharp as a two-edged sword" (5:3–4).

"A worthless man plots evil and his speech is like scorching a fire" (16:27).

"Like a lame man's legs, which hang useless, is a proverb in the mouth of fools" (26:7).

"Do you see a man who is hasty in his words? There is more hope for a fool than for him" (29:20).

Our words are always indicators of more than we intend.

When I was a young bride, someone said, "The way a woman talks about her husband in front of other people is an indicator of how she really feels about him."

This caused me to think. How did I talk about David in front of other people? It was one of my first stick-out-your-tongue examinations.

Let me see now. Ah-h-h-h-h! Well, I had to admit there was a little fuzz. Sometimes I put my husband down in groups, telling funny stories about him, beginning to practice the art of the marital verbal slam. Often I complained about him in a group of young wives. David left his stockings on the bedroom floor; he worked late too often; and on and on.

Fortunately, the symptoms of marital disrespect were in early stages and I think I diagnosed them just in time. Consequently, the treatment was simple. I began to refrain from saying things about my husband that would be demeaning to him, and I began to pray that God would give me true love for David in my heart.

It was during these years I began to learn, however, that the tongue, even when it is lying, even when it doesn't mean what it says, is devastating in what it reveals. If we will learn to listen to what we say, we will have clear indicators as to what needs to be done on this journey into spiritual maturity.

The tongue is the thermometer that shows the temperature of the inner person.

About this time I also requested that David not become proficient in telling what I call "wife jokes." I once took a Bible survey class from a college professor who was a favorite of many students. But while I admired the way he taught theology, I also noticed that he had nothing good to say about his wife. Oh, he never came right out and said, "Hey, class, my wife's a real shrew!" but his put-downs were in the form of very funny stories. "My wife did such and such; my wife says so-and-so," and the class would laugh at his clever humor. But after a while, these tales began to strike me as symptomatic. The man never said, "My wife is wonderful; she puts up with *me*. I enjoy her mind. We have good walks and talks together."

There was nothing positive in his speech about her and strangely for me, his remarkable ability of theological exposition soon dimmed.

Finally, I became embarrassed for him and I became sorry for her. I went home and pledged David not to make me the butt of his jokes, not from the pulpit, not in small social gatherings, not in the couples' Sunday school class he was teaching. And he promised and I promised and we discovered an amazing thing. Reconstructing the words that came out of our mouths about each other also helped to maintain our love for each other.

The tongue is not only the thermometer; it is often the thermostat by which we set the temperature in the inner person.

Now how about us? Time for a mouth examination—let's stick out our tongues. No protesting! I just want to see what kinds of words we normally use about the people we say we love the most. Let's say ah-h-h-h-h. Good. Uh—oh, I think there's a problem.

The tongue is coated with disaffirmation toward spouses and children; the tongue is debilitating marriages and families. We have a nag bacteria, an extremely contagious condition. Proverbs says that it is better to live in an attic than in a palace with a contentious woman. Some of us need to take a dose of Ephesians 5:28: "Even so husbands should love their wives as their own bodies. He who lives his wife loves himself."

Let's stick out our tongues; let's say ah-h-h-h-h. We must become utterly convinced that the tongue is the indicator of the person. What we talk about all the time is what we love. The words we use and the words we don't use define what we are thinking, feeling, and becoming. If we are married and we never use the pronoun *we*, we may need to examine how we are actually functioning within marital life. If there is one person about whom we say only hateful things, we need to look within ourself. Perhaps we really hate a part of ourself and are projecting that hate on the other person. If we never speak of spiritual things, doesn't this indicate a lack of spiritual thinking?

We Christians must deliberately examine what we are saying in order to discover who we really are.

We must also come to terms with the words we don't use. In the Anglican liturgy, the celebrant leads the congregation in prayers of confession of sin: "Most merciful God, we confess that we have sinned against you in thought, word, and deed, by what we have done, and by what we have left undone." In that last phrase, I often insert the words, "by what we have said and by what we have not said."

One of my regrets is a word that was not said at a time when it should have been said. An acquaintance and I had struggled through a long relationship continually in unstated conflict because of different temperaments, different value systems, and different worldviews. Out of frustration, I would pray for this individual (complaining and forgiving and finding God's heart again); I often heard the Holy Spirit whisper, I want you to be my vehicle of love to this man.

So in reluctant obedience, I mustered up fresh determination. I would write a note, make a phone call, do something kind, or say something nice. Part of the frustration on my part occurred because there was precious little in return and hardly any means by which I could measure if my efforts were appreciated—never any thanks except offhanded casual remarks and never any reaching into my life at points of need.

Then I would withdraw, sulk, complain some more, forgive again, and find the courage to head back into this one-sided relationship. One day I found him relaxed, receptive, and he did something very sweet for me. I was surprised, pleased, and in that moment, I heard an inner nudge say, Tell him that you care for him.

The inner urgency was strong, a divine compulsion that I have come to recognize instantly through years of obedience, but I had every reason in the world to disobey—he might think my interest was romantic; due to years of neglect, he had no emotional language of his own and could, therefore, easily misinterpret what I said.

As we sat together, he began to share some personal pain with me, one of the few times in our long relationship when he allowed himself to be real. Say you care about him came the insistent inner direction, but I said, "It's been wonderful spending time with you. Thank you very much. Goodbye."

I knew as soon as I left him that I had disobeyed, that there was a supernatural timing I had avoided. I went home, waited by the phone, and called him as soon as I thought he would be home; but the moment for saying the god-words was over. I had missed an opportunity to speak something into his soul that would have been healing to him at that time. And I have never had another chance to say what I should have said.

And though I have asked forgiveness, I often regret my stubborn resistance. I have learned since to speak those words of love whenever they rise in my soul regardless of the circumstances, the situation, or the personalities involved. I have learned to tell God of my weaknesses:

> We confess that we have sinned against you in thought, word and deed, by what we have done and by what we have left undone (by what we have said, and by what we have left unsaid). . .forgive us all our sins, negligences and omissions.

When Joel was little, one of the reasons it was so important for him to stick out his tongue was that he had occasional bouts with tonsillitis. Quick glimpses aided by the family flashlight showed ragged white spots spreading across his tonsils. If I could just see enough of the back of his throat, I was often able, before the temperature began raging, to whisk him quickly to the pediatrician for medication. And because of this diligence, Joel never did have to undergo a tonsillectomy; and he eventually outgrew his tendency toward tonsillitis.

The same is true regarding our speech. If we can catch our tendencies toward un-Christlike speech patterns early enough, we can go a long way toward preventing the need for major surgery.

Today it's fashionable to be foul mouthed. Our society seems to be majoring in x-rated speech. I am appalled by the language my children listen to on a daily basis in the public schools. A study of profanity at Wayne State University revealed that students used one off-color word for every fourteen. What's worse, a similar study revealed that the average adult used one off-color word for every ten.

If the tongue is the member of the body that most inadvertently reveals the condition of the soul (and if it also sets the temperature level for the inner self), what does this national verbal decline in our communal language reveal about the heart of a nation?

Some people carry their verbal monitoring too far and exclude slang, common expletives, and slightly bawdy expressions from their personal lexicon of Christian language. Colorful language often does walk a very fine line, but I would hate to exclude an occasional "drat it!" (or its equivalent) from my vocabulary for those wretched moments when that kind of exclamation is needed. What I am concerned about is obscene language, profanity, and the blasphemous use of God's name. Such usage reveals much about our personal and national values.

I remember when my grandfather and his three brothers, my great uncles, sat around and discussed the issues of the day. As a child I was enthralled by their verbal explorations. Two were day laborers, one owned a lightning rod business, and the youngest was a minister. They discussed the political parties, the policies of the presidency, the foreign issues that affected our country, and economic theories. Their discussions were often hot as each defended his view; there was laughter; there were interruptions. They talked about cars, about big business, about Marxism; they talked passionately about religion.

I'm not sure their reading extended beyond the daily paper and their listening beyond the radio news commentaries, but they could talk. They educated each other and assisted in the formation of opinions with their discussions; and while they were earthy enough to enjoy the whacky dilemmas of humanity, I never heard them use an obscene or dirty word. And the storytelling—well that's a whole other topic, and probably it's one of the reasons I feel so strongly the power of words.

I miss my old white-haired uncles, common enough in their way, who nevertheless could sit around in each other's company and intelligently discuss the issues of the day. Their minds worked.

What do old people talk about now?

How much brain growth is stimulated by investigating the contents of last night's television program? And what happens to our minds, to the actual brain matter when we are not forced to search for words, when we don't feel the passion of expressing ourselves succinctly with the right word in the right way for the right thought? Doesn't mental ability degenerate when we settle for an off-color word for every fourteen used (or for every ten)? What happens when the common man loses his intellectual capacity to discuss, to argue ideas, to fight for language, to stimulate brain cells with bright bursts of inner new word chemistry?

It is not too simplistic to emphasize that language, the use of developmental word ability, is one of the exercises that increases the capacity of the muscle known as the brain.

Furthermore, how shocking it is to hear Christians using

words that a generation ago would never have been included in the vocabularly of a hunter after holiness.

It is time for us all to say ah-h-h-h-h and to get a good look. Oh, dear. This is definitely a case of foul mouth. I know, those are just the words you use when you're with the boys—in the locker room, or with the tough-minded executives making their way up the corporate ladder. Those are just politically expedient expressions, necessary assimilation in the group environs. Yes, yes, you just use that language with the gals, close friends all, who wouldn't dream of being heard in public, just letting down your hair, being up-to-date, shocking one another for the sake of a laugh; liberated language is integral to liberated times.

One medication prescribed for foul-tongue condition in its early stages needs to be taken liberally. Start with this dose: "Let no evil talk come out of your mouths. . .And do not grieve the Holy Spirit of God" (Eph. 4:29–30).

Then take a secondary treatment if the condition is stubborn: "You shall not take the name of the LORD your God in vain: for the LORD will not hold him guiltless who takes his name in vain" (Deut. 5:11).

The tetragrammaton refers to the four consonants of the ancient Hebrew name for God (variously written JHVH, IHVH, JHWH, YHVH, YHWH) and was considered too sacred to even be pronounced. The Hebrew word *Adonai* (Lord) is substituted for this name in utterance, and the vowels of *Adonai* or *Elohim* (God) are inserted in Hebrew texts, so that modern reconstructions become Yahweh, or Jehovah.

This theological premise became suddenly clear to me when I was traveling with a study group in Jordan, Israel, and Lebanon; all of us laboring to come to some terms with the complicated and passionate causes of the Middle Eastern conflict. In Jerusalem, we were interviewing a young Jewish scholar who had emigrated to the Holy Land and become a naturalized

Israeli citizen. One of the women asked him a question and referred to God as Yahweh.

Kindly, but sternly as though restraining himself, he said, "First before I answer your question, I must explain that we would never utter that name as you have done, never speak it aloud, because it is too holy, too sacred even to be spoken." Then he went on and answered her question.

His words were a good reminder for me as to how far we have come in our journey out of holiness, when we hold nothing sacred, not even the spoken name of God. God's name is blasphemed continually; it's the aberrant punctuation mark in our modern linguistic decline. "You shall not take the name of the LORD your God in vain" is one of the Ten Commandments, and Scripture teaches that to break one of the Decalogue is to break all; they are intricately interrelated. The Christian must learn to not be casual with the name of the Almighty.

If a tongue examination reveals that we have a mouth tic that mindlessly imitates this culture's sewer-verbiage, or if our tongues suffer from a shaking palsy of sacrilege, then perhaps we should memorize the rest of that commandment, "for the LORD will not hold him guiltless who takes his name in vain." That seems to me to be strong medicine indeed.

We Christians must learn to undergo rigorous self-examination; we must honestly discern what we are really saying if we are going to understand who we are. We must begin treatment by taking daily doses of medicine when we discover white spots or a yellowish fungi on the tonsils or a blackened, fuzzy tongue.

One of the ways to undergo this examination is to end each day with a few quiet moments of reflection before the Lord whose name is so sacred that the Hebrews did not even speak it out loud. Go back over the day you have just lived and examine the words you remember speaking. Pray, "Lord, did I show any symptoms of mouth disease today? Which did I speak: life or death?"

We must listen closely to the inner reminder of this Holy Spirit. In essence, what we are doing is sticking out our tongues for the Great Physician to examine. I have found him to be most thorough in conducting examinations. If some symptoms indicate mouth disease, we must confess to him the words that were unpleasing to him and ask forgiveness. Then we should take a dose of medicine and read from those Scriptures that emphasize healthy mouth habits. We should place the medicinal verses dealing with word usage under our tongues nightly, and let them accomplish a cathartic cleansing as we sleep so that tomorrow we can begin the day with renewed strength to speak words of life.

The tongue breaketh bone, although the tongue itself have none.

John Wycliffe
Works

2

THE DIAGNOSIS
Mouth Disease

*T*he tongue—the tongue! How well I remember the chagrin I used to feel, a chagrin that had its genesis in self-conscious adolescence. I had done it again; I had talked too much. My tongue, this out-of-control muscle had spent an entire evening attempting to convince everyone that I was the most intelligent, the most charming, the wittiest person in the whole room. What on earth had I said? What verbal improprieties had I committed?

"I talk too much," I would moan later on in life to my husband, and much to my anguish he would agree with me.

The tongue—this tongue. Could nothing silence it once it got flapping? How dare it bounce against the top of my mouth! "You noticed who talked the most?" asked a friend once in the barely disguised tone of one who had obviously had enough.

One of my pet peeves is parents who explode at their children in public. The checkout counter at the grocery store seems to contain—along with chewing gum, AAA batteries, and Pillsbury cookbooks—a hidden mechanism that triggers the most outrageous verbal abuse. Bystanders are appalled by the torrent of poisonous words. Obviously, this mother (or father) has no idea of how ugly she sounds, of what a pathetic scene she is making, or of how all the sympathies of strangers are with her child (no matter how obnoxious).

Yet how often in the past I verbally abused my children. I made a point to never shame them in public, but I would have died of mortification had some of my private words been aired along with the Muzak piped into our neighborhood grocery store.

The tongue—this tongue! How often in small gatherings of church members I found myself running down the pastor—except in my case the pastor was my husband. How often I was haunted by catty or unkind things I heard my own tongue saying. *I can't believe I said that!* I would think in shame; then I would ruminate, obsessively going over and over the conversation, examining and reexamining the words I used, and creating fictional dialogue scenarios. I would rationalize and make excuses to myself about what the other person had done to trigger my negative or foolish verbiage. I simply reacted. He hit my idiot button. I was tired, defensive: I'd worked hard all day. I had a head cold and was feeling punk.

This would have been bad enough; but then I began to cast aspersions on the parties involved, even finding it necessary to justify myself in further conversations, nursing the pain caused by my own indiscretions, and not caring who else might be wounded by my misperceptions. William Blake captures this twist in his poem titled "A Poison Tree."

> I was angry with my friend;
> I told my wrath, my wrath did end.
> I was angry with my foe:
> I told it not, my wrath did grow.

And I watered it in fears,
Night & morning with my tears:
And I sunned it with smiles,
And with soft deceitful wiles.

And it grew both day and night.
Till it bore an apple bright.
And my foe beheld it shine,
And he knew that it was mine.

And into my garden stole,
When the night had veiled the pole;
In the morning glad I see;
My foe outstretched beneath the tree.

"A gentle tongue is a tree of life," says Proverbs 15:4, "but perverseness in it breaks the spirit."

Finally, when I was absolutely honest with myself, when I forced my own nose against the glass of my mirror image, I had to admit it was I who had tongue trouble. There were people I couldn't speak a positive word about; there were others to whom I could scarcely say hello; and some I had trouble looking in the eye. It was not what they did to me that was the problem; but what I said to or about them and harbored in my heart against them.

And oh, my tongue, when it got funny; that's when it was at its deadliest.

If I was going to learn to speak life and not death, if I was going to learn to use words powerfully for good in the world, I would have to come to terms with my tongue. In fact, I have since come to learn that quality tongue control is an accurate measurement of one's spiritual maturity.

Psychologists know that until a client admits his problem, there is no progress into emotional and psychological development. I finally admitted I had a problem—actually, it was much more than a problem. The apostle James accurately described my condition in chapter three of his epistle, "And the tongue is a fire. The tongue is an unrighteous world among our members, staining the whole body. . . .With it we bless the Lord and Father, and with it we curse men, who are made in the likeness of God. From the same mouth come blessing and cursing. My brethren, this ought not to be so" (vv. 6–10).

James' diagnosis was devastatingly accurate: I had mouth disease. How could I say I loved my children with one breath and then speak spitefully to them with the next? How could I honor my husband with my heart but negate him with cutting humor and slicing repartee when we were with friends? How could I say I was a follower of Christ yet speak frequently against his body, the church?

I had a mouth disease all right. Some had felt the effects of my scorching tongue, a little flame, flickering out from between my teeth, singeing here, searing there, setting little fires that others had to stamp out. Among the many verbal disorders I was to recognize throughout years of stringent self-examination, this secondary infection was early identified as *reptilia breathos*—commonly known as dragon's breath!

What's more, though James' diagnosis was accurate, his prognosis was not very hopeful. "No human being can tame the tongue—a restless evil, full of deadly poison" (v. 8). Was there no hope for my mouth disorder? Was there no antidote for the poison my tongue could spread? Was there no Fire Prevention Week that would train me how to stop my verbal pyromania?

Is there a cure for the tongue?

Well, I am taking the cure for chronic mouth disease and though the medicine is often bitter and I have been forced to readjust my speech patterns, I can testify to real progress. Months often pass without wakeful why-did-I-say-what-I-said nights. This is a major improvement. My words speak life more often than they speak death. Other people identify my progress and whisper, "Your words changed me. I am better for what you said."

Proverbs again teaches about the healing potential in our tongue, "The mind of the wise makes his speech judicious, and adds persuasiveness to his lips. Pleasant words are like a honeycomb, sweetness to the soul and health to the body" (vv. 23–24).

And yet, having undergone long mouth rehabilitation, just when I think I am in permanent remission, the symptoms of disorder appear again. David and I were traveling with friends in a car. He actually had to turn to me and say, "Karen, please don't interrupt me; you keep finishing my sentences. I can't complete my thoughts." And this after years of taking regular tongue medication.

This is disappointing, yet in my heart I know I am improving. Obviously, no researchers have discovered a permanent cure for the uncontrollable tongue, but the maintenance program I am undergoing is helping me make dramatic progress.

How has this come about?

There are several levels of treatment that I have undergone. The first level is purely functional, taking regular and sometimes daily doses of medication. I am learning to bring my mouth into obedience to the teachings on correct tongue function that I find in Scripture. Years ago, I went through the book of Proverbs and wrote out every single verse that dealt with words, with the mouth, or with the tongue. Then whenever I felt I was having an outbreak of symptoms resulting in the pain-filled, sleepless night syndrome, I would take my medicine and read and reread these verses.

I discovered that God despises the mouth disease that his children so readily tolerate. Proverbs 8:13 told me, "The fear of the Lord is hatred of evil. Pride and arrogance and the way of evil and perverted speech I hate." Proverbs 6:16–19 states, "There are six things which the Lord hates, seven which are an abomination to him: haughty eyes, a lying tongue, and hands that shed innocent blood, a heart that devises wicked plans, feet that make haste to run to evil, a false witness who breathes out lies and a man who sows discord among brothers."

The second level of treatment I underwent was surgery, both minor and major in its scope. The realization that I needed this drastic measure came from Christ's teaching, "For out of the abundance of the heart the mouth speaks. The good man out of his good treasure brings forth good, and the evil man out of his evil treasure brings forth evil" (Matt. 12:34–35). I discovered through the X-ray focus of the Holy Spirit that I had inner malignancies that needed to be removed that were actually causing my tongue to misspeak.

The third level of treatment is physical rehabilitation; my tongue is debilitated, mispronounces itself, is mute when it needs to speak, and speaks when it needs to be silent. I have undergone arduous and regular exercises that have retrained my tongue to speak in new and healthful ways.

I'm working hard at all this because I want to speak life into a dead world. I'm convinced of the power of words; they will live on after I'm gone.

In Matthew 12:36–37, Christ instructs, "I tell you, on the day of judgment men will render account for every careless word they utter; for by your words you will be justified, and by your words you will be condemned."

Christ's words about secrets being shouted upon the house-tops were adequately illustrated during the Watergate hearings when millions of Americans listened to the transcripts of taped conversations from the Oval Office of the White House. We discovered that the president and his men, to whom we had entrusted the nation's interest, had profane mouths.

That was not a moment of glee for me, to see this toppling of mighty men from their pedestals and to hear such language in the halls and rooms of power. It was a moment of shame, dishonor, and horror because this incident illuminated what will happen when our careless words are replayed in eternity.

I hold to an imaginative vision of the Great Judgment (which may be built on an appeal to unjustified guilt but which nevertheless is a what-if behavior modifier for me). All the peoples of the world have gathered before the Great White Throne. Suddenly, a deep and powerful announcement reverberates, "Karen Mains, stand forth! Karen Burton Mains, stand forth!"

Trembling and shielding my eyes against the bright light, I step out of the masses. To my dismay, I find we are being forced to listen to every word I have ever spoken.

In reality, I know my sins are covered by the blood of Christ and that every sin I have committed is forgotten in God's mind. I have no reason to fear the judgment. But the earthly struggle against this unruly member of my body, this little organ so susceptible to running-mouth virus, bids me hold onto this imaginative change agent. So I try to remember that somewhere, in some vast control room, every word uttered by the entire human race is being encoded by heavenly technocracy.

If my imaginative vision of the Judgment has even the remotest possibility of becoming true, then one day I will have to stand and listen to all the words I have ever spoken—to every nagging, complaining, jealous, boastful, whining, scheming, or secret word. If I am going to have to review every word, then I must speak words of life, words that live on, as Emily Dickinson says:

> A word is dead
> When it is said,
> Some say.
> I say it just
> Begins to live
> That day.

It is not just poets who know that words begin to live when they are said. We can all testify to them having a life of their own. Think of the harsh words spoken to you over a lifetime.

When you recall some of them, even now, a small worm gnaws and turns within. Think of the teacher who embarrassed you, long ago, in fourth grade. Think of the angry blow of words from which some marriages never recover, even after dissolution. Think of the negative brands your parents used when you were a child—Stupid! He can't do anything right! You nothing!—and of the lifetime of effort to erase their marks on soul and mind.

Words have the power to destroy. What a danger is in our mouths, these words, with this life of their own!

Yet, conversely, our tongues can speak life. Proverbs amply teaches this as well: "There is gold and abundance of costly stones; but the lips of knowledge are a precious jewel. A word fitly spoken is like apples of gold in a setting of silver. The words of the wicked lie in wait for blood, but the mouth of the upright delivers men" (20:15; 25:11; 12:6).

Now what are we to do—those of us who suspect we suffer from mouth disease? Seek a second medical opinion? We've consulted with James, but Paul also explained the symptoms clearly in his letter to the Ephesians: "filthiness, silly talk, empty words, evil talk, bitterness, wrath, anger, clamor, and slander" (5:4, 6; 4:29, 31).

Actually, there are few who don't suffer from mouth disease of some virulent strain. We all have trouble with our tongues. And one day, according to Christ, we are going to have to account for every careless word we have spoken and allow our words to justify our lives.

Yet it is within our power whether the words we speak will be words of death. The Scriptures are full of instructions regarding the kinds of words we should speak. The letter to the Ephesians, for instance, contains many verses that establish an ideal for positive verbal modification. Ephesians 5:18 says, "And do not get drunk with wine, for that is debauchery; but be filled with the Spirit, addressing one another in psalms and hymns and spiritual songs, singing and making melody to the Lord with all your heart."

Medicine for mouth disease begins by searching the Scriptures for these verses. Take a concordance and deliberately look up references listed under tongue, mouth, or speech; then write them down. This topical study approach will yield much health. Keep a running list of verses and whenever you discover a new reference to the tongue in your everyday Bible study, add it.

My mother is dead and part of the legacy that my sister and I inherited was several half-emptied prescription bottles of penicillin. Whenever I feel myself coming down with a sore throat or a fever, I pop one of the remaining tablets in the bottle. My sister is prone to sinus infections, and whenever she begins to get sick, I invariably ask, "Did you take one of mother's pills?"

We are both aware that this is medical irrationality. The tablets are so old that there is probably no medicinal effect left in them, and she and I have logically attributed the instantaneous results that we invariably experience to some sort of placebo effect—a psychological link with childhood. In fact, we have often questioned: What will we do when we run out of mother's pills?

I've concluded that I will simply procure some tiny tablets of innocuous content and put them in my bottle with its official label, "Wilma Burton; Dosage: three times daily with meals," and for the rest of my life vanquish colds and sinus infections with these placebos.

This admittedly ridiculous illustration does help to prove my point: if you have a tendency to a certain illness and there is a sure cure available, you are more likely to take the medicine than to refuse it.

The same is true of medicine for mouth disease.

Raging tongue trouble can be modified by attending to the

mouth medicine in Scripture. The Appendix of this book includes the doses from Proverbs that helped reduce my raging symptoms. The readings are divided into thirty-one sections, along with daily prayers, enough for a month of medication. If our disease has reached rampant proportions, this medicine will help. We should take a daily dose and swallow slowly so as to benefit from its full effect. If symptoms persist, we should repeat the thirty-one day cycle.

We need to get in shape in order to undergo the surgery that inevitably lies ahead for us all.

Tongue Surgeries: Minor and Major

My tongue will tell the anger of my heart:
Or else my heart concealing it will break.

Shakespeare
The Taming of the Shrew

3

MINOR SURGERY
Little Bumps That Won't Go Away

Sometimes physical examinations reveal a need for minor surgery.

Several years ago a bump appeared on the bridge of my nose. It wasn't a very big bump but it was red and hard and refused to go away. Nagged by suspicions of cancer, I hied myself to the nearest skin specialist who informed me that a minor operation would have to be performed to remove this bump on my nose that refused to go away. A date was scheduled and I was told to report to the nearby community hospital.

I honestly thought that I would sit down on a stool in an examining room, a nurse would give my nose a shot of Novocain, someone would shine a lamp on my face, the plastic surgeon would incise the skin and my tenacious little bump would pop out! A butterfly bandage would be applied and I would drive home.

Instead, I was prepped for surgery and instructed to disrobe, take off all my jewelry including my wedding rings, remove the hair pins from my hair and the makeup from my face; I was given a starched hospital gown to wear, leg warmers to pull on, and then I was swaddled in warmed blankets and tucked on a hospital dolly to be wheeled into an operating room!

Massive bright lights glared down on me, a nurse gave me a local anesthetic (the one event I had prophetically antici-pated), another nurse joined her, then my skin specialist, then the plastic surgeon. Determined not to be baffled by all this medical procedure, I made jokes on the operating table—that is, until I heard this crunching noise and realized it was the little bump on my nose protesting under the surgeon's knife. Then I began to feel faint.

The tenacious bump was finally, torturously removed. Stitches closed the incisions and I was taken to the recovery room. After a while, the skin specialist returned to report that the tissue looked benign and he would have a final report for me in a week, which was a relief but somehow made me feel all the more woozy.

"Do you have someone waiting for you?" asked the recovery room nurse, noticing how wobbly I was as I began to dress. Although she meant, "Do you have someone waiting for you in the waiting room?" I said yes. David was waiting for me at home, four miles away where he had chosen to work this morning while I "just ran over to the hospital for a while, then ran back."

As I walked to my car in the parking lot, I suddenly wished for the familiar security of my husband's firm physical presence; but then if I drove slowly, I thought, I could probably make it home.

After all, it was just minor surgery; I'd planned to fit it in between trips to the grocery store and the cleaners. I had no idea that I'd have to go to bed for the afternoon or that I'd have to honor my engagement on the South Side of Chicago that evening to speak at a formal banquet for women with a bandage on my nose and two eyes going black.

One never knows where those little bumps that won't go away will lead you.

Christ reveals unerring psychological insight; I have learned about humanity by studying his words and actions. Our Lord wisely taught what modern psychologists are attempting to investigate through clinical research studies—that words are important because of what they reveal about our inner selves. Scripture tells us that he knew what was in men's hearts. Simple obedience to Scripture and imitation of his life, even when I am not fully aware of the reasons why, invariably lead me to abundant spirituality and to emotional and psychological wholeness.

The truth is: It is impossible physiologically for any of us to speak without using our brain; and we are tripartite in our makeup, such a unity of mind, body, and soul that we cannot speak without the force of our psyche's (or the inner self's) influence.

One of the most beneficial instructions I ever received in a writing class was from a professor who understood the interplay between one's writing and the mind's replay of words. "Let your conscience be your guide. If there's a word that troubles you, if there's a phrase that bothers you every time you read it—edit, delete, change, check the spelling. Let your conscience be your guide."

What a strange approach!—attend not to the *Chicago Manual of Style,* not to Strunk and White's *The Elements of Style* (although I'm sure he wouldn't have denied their importance), but first and foremost, to one's inner sense of right and wrong word choice.

This instruction has been invaluable to me; and I find my inner voice unerringly accurate if I will but listen to it. In fact, I've added a moral dimension to my professor's advice. The more truthful I become internally, the more truthful my word choice, my idea expression, my content, my writer's voice, my style! I'm much more careful to draw on valid expert opinion, to give credit for quotes and receive permissions, to not misconstrue or manipulate other's ideas to undergird my own, and to not represent Scripture out of context. One's inner morality imposes strict integrity on the writing process.

Dorothy Sayers elaborates on the potential morality of the writing process in her book *The Mind of the Maker:*

> Now, the mere fact that the choice of the "right" word is a choice implies that the writer is potentially aware of all the wrong words as well as the right one. In the creative act, his Energy (consciously or unconsciously) passed on all the "wrong" possibilities in review as an accompaniment of selecting the right one. He may have seized immediately upon the right word as though by inspiration or he may actually have toyed with a number of the wrong ones before making the choice. . . . He is free, if he chooses, to call all or any of those wrong words into active being within his poem. . . . But the perfect poet does not do so, because his will is subdued to his idea, and to associate it with the wrong word would be to run counter to the law of his being.

As a young writer, no one ever told me that word choice may be a choice between good and evil; but as I progress in my profession, I increasingly find that writing is a moral matter, and an expression of the true condition of my inner self. Nicholas Berdyaev has written, "In the case of man, that which he creates is more expressive of him than that which he begets. The image of the artist and the poet is imprinted more clearly on his works than on his children."

Consequently, I approach my task of putting words to print with holy awe, with prayer and fasting, with self-examination, with inward contemplation, repentance, and confession.

The same is true of the words that we create in spoken

language; our true selves are transmuted in them. As we become more and more aware of our speaking mouths, our heightened consciences begin to edit, delete, and change the verbal word so that we speak truth.

Some of us have bumps on the inner person that refuse to go away and we need the Great Physician of our souls to incise these while they are still benign. This is a minor surgical process that may seem a little complicated before it is through.

Something funny happened just the other morning that illustrates this. A guest this summer was a seminarian that we had met at a Bible conference in the South and had invited to stay with us while he attended a missions conference at the nearby Christian college.

We enjoyed his companionship; as he was waiting for his ride to the airport we began to talk about romance. He expressed how hard it had been to find a young woman with the same heart for God and the things of God that he was desiring. I commiserated with him and, as encouragement, told him the story of another young friend whose fiancée had suddenly broken their engagement and within a month or two married another man.

The point of this story was that our young friend had been shocked and brokenhearted but had eventually met and married someone who was much more suited for him. In the midst of telling my tale, I made some slightly uncomplimentary remark about the young woman who had broken the engagement. "She's all honey on the outside but hard as steel on the inside," were the words I think I used.

When I finished, I noticed that the seminarian had a sheepish look on his face.

"Uh, the young woman wouldn't have been from such and such a place?" He named a city and state.

"Why yes," I replied. "I think she was."

"You don't remember her name?" he asked.

I hadn't used a name because of wanting to avoid inappropriateness, and it had slipped my memory anyway; but now I was beginning to wonder what kind of trouble my tongue had wrought. Was this the young woman's brother sitting in my living room? A kissing cousin?

The sheepish look was still on the face of the seminarian. "Was her name such-and-such?"

He got the prize. It was exactly the young woman I had been talking about. Though I hadn't used her name, I had painted her personality so clearly that a young man from across the country knew exactly who I was talking about. Fortunately, he wasn't a relative but a former boyfriend.

That definitely was a moment when I would have liked to have cut out my tongue.

The ride to the airport finally arrived; and I was left in the silence of my home to ponder a small inner bump on my soul that the Holy Spirit was casting his examining light upon. The whole scenario was not just coincidence.

In prayer, I allowed the Holy Spirit to examine this newly discovered lump. Yes, it felt hard to the touch, immovable, a lump that simply wouldn't dissolve with time. The diagnosis? Unreasonable intolerance.

Each of us has certain kinds of personalities that we just can't stand. We may be allergic to people in authority. We may find loud-talkers or life-of-the-partyers unbearable. We may have a history of distress with the opposite sex to the point where we find ourselves saying, "Oh, I prefer to be with my own sex." We may deliberately ignore the aged (they make us feel unaccountably uncomfortable). We may avoid those with physical or mental handicaps.

There is always a reason for these intolerances. If we look hard enough, we'll discover a lump on the soul somewhere.

For me, there's a certain kind of personality that is all sweetness and light on the outside but that hides the overriding force of a Mack truck on the inside. Frankly, I have trouble being charitable toward these folks. If I'm going to have to deal with a Gorgon, I want to know about it right away. No surprises please. And strangely, I have no difficulty with the strong-willed, frontal types. They are who they are; I'm married to one. I respect up-front forcefulness and through the years have learned to relate comfortably with it.

I had spoken uncharitably toward this young woman because she reminded me of a certain personality type against which I had developed a prejudice. If a woman hides a strong assertiveness behind a ruffles-and-frill personality and then uses that assertiveness when it is least expected in order to get her own way, I'm liable to experience instant negative reaction. I flip my intolerance switch.

"Well," said the Surgeon of my soul. "Do you want this lump removed? It might grow into something we would both be sorry about if we leave it."

"All right. All right." I answered, like my son Joel crawling reluctantly onto the examining table. "Take it out."

The Surgeon began to cut. "Where's your compassion?" he asked. "You certainly must realize that some people develop strong personalities that they employ manipulatively because it's the only way they know how to survive in this fallen world."

Crunch!

"Where's your pity? You must realize that many women I love have had to hide their strengths, have allowed their gifts to function underhandedly because their home, church, and society say that for a woman to be strong, to be assertive is sinful?"

Crunch! Crunch!

"And by the way, isn't the problem really that this type of personality reminds you a little too much of what you yourself have a tendency to be?"

Crunch! Crunch! Crunch!

A little wobbly, a little woozy from an operation that I thought would be quick and sweet, I recognized the bump was finally excised. Talk about lumpishness; my unreasonable intolerance grew from a characteristic in myself I disdained and against which I guarded.

Simply, I've learned the hard way that the cure for some forms of mouth disease is minor surgery. Do I hear myself redundantly excusing my tongue?—I couldn't help myself; I didn't mean what I said; I said it without thinking. A diagnosis of my inner self might indicate a hard bump growing on my soul.

Are there certain types of people about whom we always speak negatively? Do we have nothing good to say about our own sex? Do we dislike certain professions?—Lawyers are always out for our money, for instance. Is there a lump within us that won't go away?

My suggestion is that we consider minor surgery. The next time we catch our tongues flapping, we should stop, still ourselves, ask the Surgeon of the soul why we keep saying the things we keep saying. We should sit in his examining room, under the bright lamp, and let him determine whether there is a benign or malignant lump.

Our tongues often flap so much even in prayer that we don't know how to be silent when we are with the Lord. We haven't learned how to hear him speak. One of the best ways to undergo these continual examinations that must be conducted if the inner health of ourselves is to be maintained is to learn to listen in prayer.

When we are quiet before God on a regular basis, we learn to recognize the divine communication that follows time in Scripture, time in prayer, time recording our spiritual journey in a journal.

"Why do I say the things I say? Why did I say what I didn't

really mean? Why can't I help myself? Why do I major in hurtful things when I speak without thinking?"

We may not know the answers to any of these questions; but he is perfectly able to reveal the inner heart from which the mouth speaks. He can discover the inner, corroded treasure that results in outer corruption. He can uncover the hidden bitterness that is expressed by jaded humor. He can find the ragged scar tissue from old wounds that keeps you silent, makes you defensive, or inclines you toward wounding others.

Listen in silence. Ask him the whys. Then be still, attentive. The insights will come.

"For this reason," writes Paul, "I bow my knees before the Father, from whom every family in heaven and on earth is named, that according to the riches of his glory he may grant you to be strengthened with might through his Spirit in the inner man, and that Christ may dwell in your hearts through faith; that you, being rooted and grounded in love. . .may be filled with all the fullness of God" (Eph. 3:14–19).

The cause for tongue disease is really dis-ease in the heart and sometimes the only cure is a surgical measure, a cutting out of the little bumps that won't go away.

"Then you should say what you mean," the March Hare went on.

"I do," Alice hastily replied; *"at least—at least I mean what I say—that's the same thing, you know."*

"Not the same thing a bit!" said the Hatter.

Lewis Carroll
Alice's Adventure in Wonderland

4

LIES

The Ones I'm Never Going to Tell Again

Sometimes divine surgery is a matter of cutting away the ugly warts I call intentional lies. I've told a lot of lies in life, most of which I've painfully learned not to repeat. The very first lie I remember telling was when I was about four or five and my mother introduced a forbidden fruit. She told me I was not to play with the Mercurochrome.

Despite this prohibition, on one of the days when we were caring for my apple-cheeked two-year-old cousin Barbara, I spilled the Mercurochrome while liberally dousing Barbara's imaginary wounds. Horrified, I watched the orange and pink liquid eat into the top of the new sewing machine cabinet. I hid the sticky evidence underneath a linen dresser cloth with the disintegrating varnish immediately adhering to the fabric.

Mother discovered the empty Mercurochrome bottle before she discovered the fabric bonded to her sewing machine cabinet. "What happened to this?" she asked, accusation rising in her tone.

"Oh," I replied, disingenuously, "Barbara drank it." Barbara had gone home and wasn't around to defend herself; and since no word had come of her early demise, mother made light of the issue. I feel inclined to say that my mother was a very intelligent woman, but a poet; somehow logical connections didn't come as rapidly for her as they did for my father—he always knew when I was lying.

At any rate, I don't remember being punished for disobeying or for lying; the incident was probably forgotten in the urgency of the next poetic birthing. But the great white blister on the top of the cabinet stirred my tender conscience, and I ruefully remembered my fall from innocence each time I looked at it.

Being for a long while an only child used to exclusive attention, I lied when my cousin Jerry caused a major hullabaloo by being bitten by a dog in Des Moines, Iowa, the Burton clan's city of residence. My parents and I were on a stopover from Chicago to meet my grandparents and then to continue on a camping trip with them to California. In Denver, I told my mother I had been bitten too (hoping, I suppose, for the same attentive hullabaloo). She believed me. Dad and my grandparents continued their trip as mother and I waited for word from the Iowa State Police as to the rabid condition of the dog.

I lied when I told my fourth grade class that my grandfather had bought me a horse (and I lied again when close classmates pinned me about why I never before had mentioned such a fabulous prize); and I lied again when I informed them later, finding my spontaneous fabrication increasingly difficult to maintain, that the horse had died.

The first kind of lie with which I had to deal is the intentional lie, the lie I know I am telling.

One of the ten commandments bears this prohibition, "You shall not bear false witness against your neighbor" (Exod. 20:16). Ephesians 4:25 says, "Therefore, putting away falsehood, let everyone speak the truth with his neighbor." Colossians 3:9 repeats, "Do not lie to one another, seeing that you have put off the old nature with its practices."

The cure for intentional lies is a deliberate cutting away of the warts of untruth—minor surgery. We must learn to do what we know to do. We cannot stretch the truth, color it, be inexact in what we report, emotionally freight information to our own advantage. We must bring our mouth into obedience to what Scripture insists upon regarding speaking the truth, and we must learn to apologize when we have uttered untruths, and if necessary, ask forgiveness. We must obediently submit to the Holy Spirit as he excises these little bumps.

Hans Christian Anderson has written a wonderful little tale titled "It's Absolutely True!"

> It was a chicken-house at the other end of the town. The sun went down, and the hens flew up. One of them was a white short-legged bird, who regularly laid her eggs and then preened herself. While doing this one day a feather came loose and went fluttering down. "So much for that one!" she said. "The more I preen, the lovelier I shall grow, no doubt!" Of course it was only said in fun, because she was the fun-maker among the hens, though in other ways, (as you've just heard) most respectable. After that, she went off to sleep.
>
> All about was quite dark; hen sat with hen, but the one next to her was still awake. She had heard, and had not heard—as you must often do in this world, if you are to live in peace and quiet. And yet she couldn't help saying to the hen perched on the other side of her, "Did you hear that? I give no names, but there is a hen who means to pluck out her feathers for the sake of her looks. If I were a cock, I'd simply despise her."
>
> Now directly above the hens sat the owl, with her owl husband and her owl children. They had sharp ears in that family; they could hear every word their hen neighbor said; and they rolled their eyes, and the owl mother fanned

herself with her wings, "Don't take any notice—but of course you heard what she said, didn't you? I heard it with my own ears, and they're going to hear a lot before they drop off. One of the hens has so far forgotten what is fit and proper for a hen that she's calmly plucking out all her feathers in full view of the cock."

"Prenez garde aux enfants!" said the father owl. "Not in the children's hearing."

"But I must tell the owl over the way; she's so highly respected in our set." And away flew the mother.

"Tu-whit, to-who!" they both hooted, and it carried right down to the doves in the dovecot across the yard. "Have you heard, have you heard? To-who! There's a hen that's plucked out all her feathers for the sake of the cock. She'll freeze to death, if she isn't dead already, tu-who!"

"Where, ooh, where?" cooed the doves.

"In the yard opposite. I as good as saw it with my own eyes. Really the story's almost too improper to repeat; but it's absolutely true!"

"Tru-rue, tr-rue, every wor-rd!" said the doves; and they cooed down to their hen-run, "There's a hen, some say there are two, who have plucked out all their feathers so as to look different from the others and to attract the attention of the cock. It's a risky thing to do; suppose they catch cold and die of fever. . .yes, they're dead—two of them."

Then the cock joined in: "Wake up, wake up!" he crowed and flew up on to the wooden fence. His eyes were still sleepy, but he crowed away all the same; "Three hens have died of love for a cock; they had plucked out all their feathers. It's a horrible story—I don't want it—pass it on! Pass it on, pass it on!" And so the story flew from one hen-house to another, till at last it came back to the place where it had really started.

"There are five hens"—that's how it ran—"who have all plucked out their feathers to show which of them had got thinnest for love of the cock. Then they pecked at each other till the blood came and they all fell down dead, to the shame and disgrace of their family and the serious loss of their owner."

The hen that had lost the one loose little feather didn't of course recognize her own story and, as she was a respectable hen, she said, "How I despise those hens!—though there are plenty more just like them. That's not the kind of thing to be hushed up, and I shall do my best to get the story into the papers, so that it may go all over the country. It'll serve those hens right and their family too."

And into papers it came—all there in print—and it's absolutely true: "One little feather can easily become five hens!"

And it's absolutely true that one little misconception can grow into a web of lies until the real can't be distinguished from the fantasy. A massacre can grow from a minor bump. Reality always dims when Liar, in any of his disguises—braggart, dissembler, jokester—becomes our friend.

One of the ways we befriend lies is to use words in ways that tangle their true meanings. We develop modern jargon that is less morally incriminating. Sexual immorality becomes "alternative lifestyles." Pornography is labeled "realism." Abortion becomes "terminated pregnancy." Language has the potential for clear communication, or it has the potential to mangle and manipulate meaning.

"I wasn't angry, just a little peeved," we might say, not wanting to identify or to have others identify our true emotions. In truth, we were angry and need to admit to ourselves what actually was. Saying one thing, but acting and meaning something else has the potential for creating life systems that are warped, harmful, if not even evil. We need to develop the habit of asking about our own words, "Was that absolutely true?"

"Let your yea be yea; let your nay be nay," says Christ (Matt. 5:37 KJV). Be true to your word.

It has been helpful for me to define neuroticism as that

tendency to want to say yes and no at the same time. One of our children had a marvelous method of pulling me ring-around-the-rosy in his verbal circles: "I want to clean up my room but I can't because I don't have any help; but my room is so much of a mess that I don't want anyone to touch my stuff, so I can't clean it up even though I want to."

Or how about this primitive neurosis displayed at bath time? My child wanted out; but when I took him out, he cried to go back in the tub. When I put him back in the water, he cried to get out.

Early warning wisdom will help parents to teach their children to say yes when they mean yes and say no when they mean no. You cannot have no and yes at the same time. You cannot say one thing and mean another.

The adult is also a victim of the neurotic ring-a-lievio, the captured player trapped in the middle of the circle: I want to do something; but I'm afraid I'll fail, so I don't want to do it as well—yes/no, no/yes, yes/no.

We have to catch ourself in the middle of the neurotic words because of their inclination to grow out of proportion, and control us. If we want something, we should get it; if we can't have it, we should stop whining about it. We must decide. We can't allow regrets. Is what we say absolutely true?

George Fox's *Journal* is a religious classic of that same spiritual genre of writings as Augustine, John Wesley, Madame Guyon, and George Whitefield. Fox brought religious renewal to England through the founding of the Society of Friends (Quakers) during the Commonwealth period of 1640–1660. The basic truth that Fox spread was that all men and women have access within themselves to communion with the divine. As J. Elton Trueblood wrote about Fox, "He learned to experience the life of Christ in the Present Tense." The 1600s were a time of much political unrest and religious foment in which many bands of religious dissenters formed but eventually faded away. The Friends, however, influenced their world in ways disproportionate to their actual numbers.

Members of the Society of Friends regularly found themselves forced to choose between religious conscience and acts of civil disobedience. Hauled before magistrates for joining together in worship, they refused to take oaths, obeying literally Christ's words, "Swear not. . .neither by heaven. . .nor by the earth. . .but let your communication be, Yea, yea; Nay, nay" (Matt. 5:34–37 KJV); and they were jailed in the rankest of prisons.

Fox's *Journal* is filled with records of his own personal arrests, trials, and jailings. After being jailed in Lancaster prison, Fox was again brought before a tribunal:

> I told them I could not take any oath at all, because Christ and His Apostle had forbidden it; and they had sufficient experience of swearers, first one way, then another; but I had never taken any oath in my life.
>
> Then Rawlinson asked me whether I held it was unlawful to swear. This question he put on purpose to ensnare me; for by an Act that was made those were liable to banishment or a great fine that should say it was unlawful to swear. But I, seeing the snare, avoided it, and told him that "in time of the law amongst the Jews, before Christ came, the law commanded them to swear but Christ, who doth fulfill the law in His gospel-time, commands not to swear at all; and the apostle James forbids swearing, even to them that were Jews, and had the law of God."
>
> After much discourse, they called for the jailer, and committed me to prison.

One may not agree with this literal interpretation of Christ's word for which these Christians chose to suffer; but one can't help but admire the obedience to Christ's light as shown to one's inner conscience. And one can't help but wonder what kind of a culture this world would become if the same stress on the truth of a man's or woman's word was cherished.

In another exchange before a judge, Fox writes: "I said, 'Our Yea is yea, and our Nay is nay'; and if we transgress our yea and our nay, let us suffer as they do, or should do, that swear falsely."

To make sure we understand the imprisonment to which these people knew they were being sentenced, it would be well worth reading a few more lines from Fox's *Journal:*

> I was put into a tower where the smoke of the other prisoners came up so thick it stood as dew upon the walls, and sometimes it was so thick that I could hardly see the candle when it burned; and I being locked under three locks, the under-jailer, when the smoke was great, would hardly be persuaded to come up to unlock one of the uppermost doors for fear of the smoke, so that I was almost smothered.
>
> Besides, it rained in upon my bed, and many times, when I went to stop out the rain in the cold winter-season, my shirt was as wet as muck. . .and the place being high and open to the wind. . .
>
> In this manner, I lay all that long, cold winter till the next assize, in which time I was so starved, and so frozen with cold and wet with the rain that my body was greatly swelled and my limbs much benumbed.

Would that the church today had one-quarter of the commitment to suffer for the sake of truth.

After the intentional lie, the next level is the lie of self-negligence. These untruths spring from not caring enough about ourselves to get to know who we really are. When we were in the pastorate and raising four small children, I used to say, "I don't have enough time to get organized; I don't have enough time to develop a devotional life." One day I decided I would see if that was true. I developed a time log and charted every minute of the way I spent my time for the next two weeks. I discovered I had enough time to watch hours of television, time to read indiscriminately, time to chat with neighbors, and absolute hours of mental "wool-gathering" for which I couldn't account.

I had the time; I just wasn't using my time well. One of the children dropped the portable television set and instead of having it repaired, we junked it. That saved me (according to the national average) an estimated forty-four hours per week.

Another phrase I heard myself repeating was, "I don't have enough energy." Determining whether this phrase was true or not took me into an exciting journey of self-knowledge.

All my life I've prided myself on being a people person—the more the merrier, a crowd at all times, as many kids of our own as we could afford to have, people coming and going, people living with us, people, people, people. The fatigue I felt from all this activity I attributed to a low energy level and to bad time and resource management.

Fatigue has been my greatest enemy, and I have fought against it with raw-boned determination. I refused to give in to it. Just because I had to go to bed for two days after a dinner party for sixteen wouldn't mean that I wouldn't invite another sixteen next week. I've prayed against this fatigue, have cried over it, have taken vitamins, have changed my eating habits, have tried to exercise as much as possible, and adamantly have pushed myself to keep up all personal ministry contacts.

The fact that for some thirty-five years I thought I was a people person has been a lie of negligence.

Please don't misunderstand me. I love people, but generally, after extended conversation, I'm exhausted. For instance, a Bible conference week of answering questions, asking questions, and counseling after the speaking sessions normally meant that I would go home, collapse, and probably come down with a cold.

The lie of negligence I was attempting to live out was that I was an *extroverted* people-lover. What the Holy Spirit has been attempting to teach me is that I am in *introverted* people-lover.

In their book *Please Understand Me: Character and Temperament Types,* the authors David Kiersey and Marilyn Bates define the difference between the categories of extroversion and introversion in this way:

> Extroverts with their need for sociability, appear to be energized, or tuned up by people. Talking to people, playing with people, working with people is what charges their batteries.
>
> While the extrovert is sociable, the introvert is territorial. That is, he desires space: private places in the mind and private environmental places. Introverts seem to draw their energies from a different source than do extroverts; pursuing solitary activities, working quietly alone, reading, meditating, participating in activities which involve few or no other people.

This explained a lot. Being introverted or extroverted has nothing to do with whether or not you like people, relate easily with them, or enjoy their company. It has everything to do with the source from which you draw your strength.

This self-understanding has given me the courage to build into my life activities that renew me. I write and become strong. I read when I become fatigued. I allow myself quiet spaces after intensive people times. Long walks and times of memorization cure my blahs. Quiet, solitude, silence—these are my well-loved companions. And not only am I healthier than I have ever been, I am becoming physically stronger too.

We must come to terms with the intentional lies in our lives, we must allow and hold sacred the veracity of our yeses and noes, and we must deal with the lies of self-negligence. We must develop a passionate love affair with truth. Again, one simple way to do this is to develop an interior systems check that continually asks, "What am I saying, and is it absolutely true?"

This is minor surgery, a cutting away of the little bumps and warts that can grow into more serious problems—like those lies we don't know we are telling.

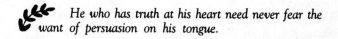 *He who has truth at his heart need never fear the want of persuasion on his tongue.*

William Wetmore Story

5

MAJOR SURGERY
The Lies I Didn't Know I Was Telling

$R.$ D. Laing has written a logical knot that includes a powerful truth.

> The range of what we think and do—
> Is limited by what we fail to notice;
> And because we fail to notice,
> That we fail to notice—
> There is little we can do to change
> Until we notice how failing to notice
> Shapes our thoughts and deeds.

Fyodor Dostoyevski, the great Russian writer, says the same thing in a different way in his book *Notes from the Underground.* "Every man has reminiscences which he would not tell to everyone but only to his friends. He has other matters in his mind which he would not reveal even to his friends, but only to himself and that in secret. But there are other things which a man is afraid to tell even to himself, and every decent man has a number of such things stored away in his mind."

The psalmist writes, "Clear thou me from hidden faults. Keep back thy servant from presumptuous sins; let them not have dominion over me! Then I shall be blameless, and innocent of great transgression" (Psalm 19:12–13).

Psychologists call these hidden faults lacunae, that is, matters we hide away, fail to notice, and are afraid to tell even ourselves.

Webster's defines a lacuna as a ditch, a hole, a cavity, a space where something has been omitted or has come out, a gap. These hidden faults are gaps in our self-understanding, but they can often be such powerful gaps that they act like black holes in the soul that suck up us and those we love.

Hidden faults are not simply overlooked areas of error, but they are whole inner systems that we devise to keep ourselves from looking at painful truth. These are the lies we don't know we are telling.

Scripture is forceful about the need for the inner man to be whole. The psalmist writes again in Psalm 51:6, "Behold thou desirest truth in the inward being; therefore teach me wisdom in my secret heart."

A hidden fault is self-deception and is different than the techniques of repression, denial, reversal, and rationalization because it is often a combination of all these defensive mechanisms and results in subconscious denial of reality.

Hidden faults can be extremely dangerous—they are the stuff of which human disaster is made. My husband, David, and I saw the Greek play *Antigone* by Sophocles this summer. One major theme of Greek tragedy is the sorry chain of events begun by a slight flaw in character at the outset of the drama. One wrong decision made on the part of the hero or heroine at the beginning of the play leads to total and irrevocable downfall. Empires fall. Families are destroyed. Dynasties tumble.

In short, Antigone is the daughter of the dead king Oedipus. After her brothers Eteocles and Polyneices had killed each other in the war of the Seven Against Thebes, her uncle, King Creon, forbade anyone to bury Polyneices' body because he had attacked his own city. Antigone, horrified, defies the royal edict, buries her brother, and is condemned to death for this defiance by being sealed in a cave. Haemon, the king's son, who loves Antigone, eventually takes his life before the eyes of his horrified father; and when his mother hears of his death, she commits suicide as well.

Finally Creon cries, "Purblind sin of mine! There is no absolution / For perversity that dragged a son to death. . ." The Leader answers, "Late, too late, your reason reasons right!"

Some of the saddest lines in literature are at the end of this play:

> Where wisdom is, there happiness will crown
> A piety that nothing will corrode.
> But high and mighty words and ways
> Are flogged to humbleness, till age,
> Beaten to its knees, at last is wise.

Because of hidden faults, there are many Greek tragedies being played out in the lives of Christians I know. Perhaps, a Christian leader has such a hidden need for recognition and approval, that he imposes upon his followers a growth scheme that is so grandiose that it takes millions of dollars and countless hours to fulfill. And because he or she is a gifted person of unusual charisma, his or her followers make sacrifices for the sake of his or her cause.

For the sake of illustration, there may be no need in the kingdom for a Christian camping center in the middle of New York City or a Christians' only shopping mall with Christian merchants, marketing experts, designers, maintenance crew, and buyers, yet incredible sums are diverted from the greater work of the kingdom for causes not unlike these. When this man or woman's grandiose plan is finally fulfilled, he or she is insatiably satisfied and claims it was done in the name of faith. What follows is one presumptuous plan after another until the reach exceeds the grasp, and the whole Christian empire that has been built tumbles. Bank foreclosures occur. Bankruptcy is declared. Marriages break beneath the strain. Fellow Christians are disillusioned. Some of the weaker ones cast away their faith. Young Christians who have known this master schemer's moral shenanigans leave the church out of desperation.

This is modern Greek tragedy—a hidden flaw in one man's soul leads to the downfall of an earthly empire constructed in the name of God, which then sucks many into the black hole of itself.

Hannah Arendt, the social philosopher, while writing about the Holocaust maintained that the mix of self-deception and free will allows man to do evil, believing it good. And so throughout the centuries, witchhunts, heresy trials, and the burning of saints at the stake have been conducted in the name of Christ, with such shams being nothing more than evil parading itself in the garments of godliness. Abraham Kuyper writes in *To Be Near Unto God*, "Sin propagates itself nowhere more rapidly than in Religion."

Personal authenticity means that my inward self and my outward self are one. I am who I am when with family, friends, the public, and ultimately with God. By insisting on inner reality, and outward transparency, I mirror the image of who God intends and created me to be. My tongue then reflects this personal integrity.

But I know my most human proclivities. I am like the psalmist; I cry, "Clear thou me from hidden faults. Keep back thy servant from presumptuous sins; let them not have dominion over me. Then I shall be blameless, and innocent of great transgression" (19:12–13).

The greatest transgressions are poisonous flowers, rank and putrid, springing up from the underground decay of each man's and woman's soul. Because we choose not to notice the deadly flowers of this dark garden, they have dominion over us, and they then lead us to acts and words of incredible human presumption.

Hidden faults are the reason a Christian leader can leave his spouse, live with another partner, also a Christian; and while both of them are waiting for their divorces, this person testifies to the fact that he has never loved his first spouse more. After the divorces are final, he and the new partner will begin a ministry for the divorced. (This, tragically, is not fiction.)

These hidden faults, the lies we live out without knowing them, are the things a man is afraid to tell even to himself but which are stored tightly away in the deep mind. So how do we come to terms with the hidden faults that by their very nature are hidden?

The children's game of pickup sticks is a good illustration of one approach. In this game, multicolored sticks are allowed to fall randomly in a pile. The players must lift the sticks off the pile without moving any of the other sticks. If one moves, the player forfeits his turn to the next player. Points are earned by the number and color of the sticks that are moved off the pile, and this can be a laborious process.

Now, of course, the sticks in the deep center of the pile can't be moved until the easier ones on top are flipped away. One stick at a time is taken off the pile until, finally, the ones in the deepest center are able in their turn to be removed.

I think it's the same way with hidden faults. We remove the errors we can see—lies of negligence, lies of intent—and it's not until these are removed that we can come to terms with the sticks that are hidden underneath. This deep awareness is brought about by the probing of the Holy Spirit, an exploratory surgery we allow him to conduct in order to discover the illness in our most inward selves.

Hidden faults affect our actions and our verbalizations. A

woman friend of mine, happily married but approaching middle age, began to have sudden attractions for younger men. "I knew something was wrong when a salesman spent a little extra time laughing and shooting the breeze with me and I thought about him all the next day. I really knew something was wrong when a man from our church came to my husband and myself for some marital counseling and all I could do was think about him and drop his name into all possible conversations!"

When she looked within, using the prayer of listening, she saw she had endured a long pattern of male neglect. Her father had been emotionally distant; her older brother in early years had considered her a pest and was still aloof as an adult; she had several broken romances; and her husband had a tendency to become overinvolved in his work, his hobbies, and his sports activities.

"I was hungry for male attention, so starved that I could become enamored of a passing salesman." My friend decided this could lead to tragedy. She got counseling, had some frank conversations with her husband, learned to experience the healing love of the male Christ, began a correspondence with her brother, and established healthy friendships with Christian men in a couples Bible study group.

Most of us don't come to terms with the sins in our lives quite as productively as this friend of mine. Our own hidden faults are often the reason we have complaining tongues, never can say I love you, find it impossible to affirm the people we care for the most, become compulsive in our phone conversations, spill anger inappropriately, accuse others incessantly, major in verbal trivia, and can't stop talking about ourselves.

How do I know? Because this is exactly the work the Lord has been doing in me over the last years. Together we've worked on the sticks on the top of the pile, and now I'm amazed at what hidden faults the Holy Spirit is revealing to me. I'm learning the tragic truth that hidden faults keep others from seeing the truth—Christ in us; and because our inner selves influence our outer verbalizations, we keep others from hearing Christ's words when we speak.

Sometimes the lacunae of the soul cause us to create whole fictions within which we attempt to live and to force the ones we love to live. I know this all too well.

Part of the estate that needed to be settled after the death of both of my parents was a ninety-acre farm in Waterman, Illinois. My father had been restoring this piece of land for his retirement. Most people who saw the old farmhouse recommended that the quickest way to restore it would be to call in bulldozers, but my father loved to work with his hands. He took delight in shoring up the sagging floors, stripping woodwork, putting on new roofs, and planning additions.

The bathroom alone was symbolic of the whole. The shower head was at the wrong end of the tub. Instead of the drain being under it, the drain was at the opposite end, and the floor slanted away from the drain—all a little unhandy when it came time to pull the plug.

Some people might have called the farmhouse a "handyman's dream"; my father certainly thought so. For the rest of the world, clear-eyed realists all, it was a nightmare come true, a real-life version of the once popular country tune "This Ol' House."

Needless to say, I had strong emotional ties to that crazy house and the beautiful land where my father had planted the orchard and to the rolling pasture with its muddy creek from which my children invariably returned wet and filthy with bloodsuckers clinging to their bare legs. More gym shoes were lost and ruined in the creek than I care to count.

Bloodsuckers aside, the farm had provided my children and myself with the rich and fertile stuff of good memories. To sell the farm meant cutting myself off from all these associations, and I kept hearing my dad say, "Never sell the farm."

My brother, who was the executor of my parent's will, can testify to how frequently I vacillated. One day—sell; the next day—don't sell.

Finally, I constructed an elaborate solution. The tillable land really didn't mean anything to me. It was the front fourteen acres that had provided those idyllic weekends (at least those Fridays and Saturdays when David, in the pastorate at the time, was absorbed with his sermon preparations). And this was the part of the farm my father had worked the hardest to improve.

We would sell the back part of the farm and divide the inheritance with my brother and sister; then I would use my share to purchase those fourteen front acres. We would fix up the old farmhouse just enough to make it habitable for family getaways; and, eventually, we would sell our home in town and build high on the slope in the pasture with a view of the land for miles around. We could have a stable and horses, the chicken coop I've always wanted, and get back into keeping bees.

In the midst of all this planning, David and I had dinner with a friend; and when I shared my thinking about the farm, she only asked one question, "How far away is the farm?"

David answered, "Oh, about two hours."

The farm was all of forty-five minutes away, at the most one hour, from our house. All my kids could have accurately told the distance to the farm, but David really didn't know.

I lay awake that night, just as I had so many nights before scheming and dreaming; but I kept hearing his words, and I began to face cold reality.

The next morning I discovered some discrepancy in our viewpoints as to how many times David had visited the farm in the twenty some years my parents owned it. David's count was at least twenty; mine was no more than a half-dozen times. At any rate, David hadn't gone out there enough to know the correct answer to the question, "How far away is the farm?"

The truth, the simple truth had to be faced: David did not hold any passionate feelings for the farm.

So what did this mean? It meant I was creating an elaborate fiction in which I would soon expect my entire family to live.

David's not a gardener. I'm the one who feels rapturous about tractors, country fairs, and grapes ripening in the sun on the vine. I love the smell of manure in barns; my husband has to be coerced out of his business suits into jeans. Where in the world did I get the idea that once we bought the farm, he would love bib overalls and workboots?

I'm the one who wanted the farm; I wanted the memories of the happy days spent rising early with my parents, my father's laughter, and my mother's wonderful garden beans cooked down in a pot with hamhocks and boiled potatoes. I wanted to keep the place where I had heard the silent echo of my young children's laughter simply by walking under the old and disorderly apple trees on the front lawn. I wanted the wind over the cornfields, the thick tangle of elderberry bushes, and hot summer days when a slight breeze rustled the leaves of the old cottonwoods at the end of the driveway.

I wanted robber death to go away and leave me at least with memories.

As the cold light of reality dawned upon me, I realized that because of David's love for me, he was allowing my strong, inordinate emotional attachment to overcome his better judgment. Not only that, this fiction would have been disastrous in terms of time, energy, and finances, and it would have detracted from our commitment to the kingdom of God.

There's nothing wrong with restoring a farm, except if it competes with one's major divine calling. In my case, that means writing redemptive literature, true fiction that uses true words to reveal Christ and bring spiritual healing.

In David's case, a divine calling means reminding a nation of its need for spiritual regenesis and creating a hunger for classical spiritual revival. How crafty the Enemy of our soul is, and how eagerly he uses our inner flaws, the hidden untruths, our inordinate needs to control us in ways of which we are unaware and to keep us from the work of God.

When I shared this incident with a friend, she laughed. Just that week she had discovered a fiction of her own creating. Raised in an emotionally deprived background, she discovered that the house she was attempting to buy was too important to her. "I wanted it to be the home I never had as a child, and I was willing to pay any price and make any sacrifice to achieve it."

Cold truth dawned: all I could talk about was the farm, but David didn't even know how far away it was. I turned to the Lord and prayed, "Forgive me for trusting more in my earthly father's inheritance than in my heavenly father's inheritance. Help me to believe that it is you who in the days ahead will provide me and my children and my grandchildren with the rich emotional loam from which memories and family times are formed. Amen."

We must learn to notice the things we have failed to notice so that they will not shape our thoughts, words, and deeds. I do not want to be flogged to humbleness, beaten to my knees, and aged; I want to be authentic, wise, well before that time.

A sharp tongue is the only edged tool that grows keener with constant use.

Washington Irving

6

JAMESIAN FICTIONS

While thinking about the whole topic of self-deception and while examining my own inner flaws, I decided to look at scriptural personalities to see if any had black holes in their souls that forced them to create whole fictions in which they attempted to live. Eve's fiction was that she believed she could be like God. Adam's fiction was that he didn't have to take responsibility for his own sinful actions. Consequently, the idyllic Eden was spoiled. Chaos chased itself in the garden. Flaming angels barred entrance to the one true utopia that ever was.

The Old Testament chronicle of human fictions continues: Lot deceived himself into thinking that he could live near corruption without being tainted. Abraham and Sarah created a whole drama of tragedy when they grew impatient with God's long delayed promise. They pretended that they could substitute a misbegotten heir without setting irrevocable consequences into order. Isaac fooled himself into thinking that parental favoritism would have no family effect. Jacob, the schemer, deluded himself into believing he could force God's hand by himself.

The presence of an overwhelming universality of self-deception in the lives of all the patriarchs indicates that it is a basic human condition. We have self-deceptions that hide in the dark caverns of our inward person. I have self-deceptions unknown to me, and if we are not careful, we will attempt to create fictions within which it will be impossible to live.

A closer look at one New Testament character may give us a broad enough sample to understand how this tendency to self-deceive works and to what it can lead us.

Sons of thunder! Who do you know that reminds you of a son of thunder? Impetuosity, bombastic expression, men or women of action, movers and shakers, people with short fuses. This was Christ's nickname for two of his apostles, the brothers James and John, sons of Zebedee. Of what was he thinking when he gave this appellation? Is it a clue to the fiction that I suspect one of the brothers, James, began creating in his own life?

I think James' own particular unreality began close to the moment when he received his call from Christ to be a fisher of men instead of a catcher of fish. Yes, Jesus had filled their nets, miraculously; but besides this powerful display, what were James' motives for leaving fishing? Were they all altruistic? People's motives seldom are. We can only guess why James left his nets, but some of the mixed motives I might have had are: (1) simply to get away from all those stinking fish and that hard physical labor; (2) to escape from the domination of my father Zebedee; (3) to suspect, that at least, here was my one slim chance for glory; and (4) to achieve some prestige by association with this young teacher so filled with charisma that all Galilee was buzzing about him and whom the prophet John had declared to be a somebody.

James, of course, is an eyewitness to all the healing miracles of Christ and somewhere in here his fiction begins to form out of the undefined psychological need of his own inner self. Perhaps he was hungry for recognition, for significant position—whatever; my premise is that he begins to mistake spiritual power for human success. He begins to measure the unknown in terms of the known. His measurements are status, popularity, renown, political revolt, and instantaneous results.

He has no idea that supernatural achievement is only attained by learning through failure, suffering, brokenness—crosses.

James is impressed with the prerogatives implied in the title "apostle." Christ has now chosen him to be one of the inner band; and more and more frequently, he finds himself, with his brother John and with Simon Peter, privy to the inner confidences of Christ. He's special to Christ, he and his brother and Peter, more special than any of the others. There's a divine appointment upon his life, a destiny ahead for him.

Soon, as an itinerant evangelist, at his very word, demons are cast out, and he has the actual authority to cure diseases. James becomes intoxicated with the exercise of power. And he ceases to respond to the truth and begins to make his own truth. He witnesses the spectacular on the Mount of Transfiguration; but soon after Christ's remarkable transformation, Scripture tells us that the disciples came to the Lord wondering, "Who is the greatest in the kingdom of heaven?" (Matt. 18:1).

I suspect that the question was asked because there had been much discussion regarding office, future position in the coming kingdom, rank, superiority of ability, leadership potential; and I imagine that the two sons of thunder had somewhat to do with all this premature strategizing. I imagine this because of the favor their mother asked of Christ.

I've always liked Zebedee's wife, James and John's pushy mother; she actually embodied the modern stereotypes of the Jewish mother, ambitious for the advancement of her children, her sons the kingdom makers. She said to Christ, "Command that these two sons of mine may sit, one at your right hand and one at your left, in your kingdom" (Matt. 20:21). Now this woman has no small ambitions. But I always wonder as I read her words, "Who put her up to it?"

I think I know.

Why do I suspect that James is creating an exalted fiction for himself?

Partly because of the things "unsaid," the verbal vacuums, the spoken evidences that would indicate understanding. This lack indicated denial. Christ had been teaching all along about his death and his resurrection. His teaching concepts about what the kingdom of God is like continually reinforce the truth about dying to oneself, picking up one's cross, laying down one's life, being leaders who are also servants.

In order to be deaf to this much truth, one had to be creating one's own preferred truth, and this springs out of one's own psychological need, inordinate affections, strong human desires.

James wanted that spiritual power so badly he could taste it, sharp and aspiring on his tongue. He wanted to rule. He wanted thousands to come and hear him preach. He wanted human acclamation, his name spoken in the marketplace. He wanted to be Christ's number one confidant. John could package the mystical teachings, could popularize this message for the masses. Peter, with his attractive, crowd-pleasing macho magnetism could be the public figurehead. But he, James, the son of Zebedee, would be Christ's right-hand advisor, the power behind the throne.

Together they would usher in the kingdom of God with spiritual fireworks, with healing services that would astound. This kingdom would rival—no, no—it would *surpass* Rome. And if there was any disagreement or any resistance, they would just call down fire from heaven!

Am I surmising too much? Remember the Samaritan village

that wouldn't receive Christ? Remember that it was James and John who spoke, "Lord, do you want us to bid fire come down from heaven and consume them?" (Luke 9:54). The tongue always tells.

Ah, here is spiritual authority gone whacky. Here is presumption. Here is self-deception. Here is hidden fault. Here is a fiction that bodes a mighty delusion.

I feel like I know James. My husband and I are involved in public ministry. Through the years I've watched fellow ministers succumb to the temptations inherent in spiritual annointing, in divine favor. The seductions are many and subtle. Through the years I've been witness to the tug of war in my own heart.

It's easy to determine spiritual success by human measurements—by the amount of mail in the mailroom, by the number of radio outlets that beam your program across the nation. It's easy to assume that God's work can't be moved along without your particular genius. It's easy to be seduced by the Christian bestseller lists, to think that you're God's right-hand person because you've equated spiritual power with numbers.

This exact thinking has been the downfall of many a James whose spiritual fiction brought him to the point where he really believed he could exercise capricious judgment, call down fire from heaven on dissenters. But oh, the awakening that comes, the cold harsh dawnings of reality when suddenly, like James, we confront the cross. Death lears. There's an agony too that is part of the Kingdom. It's not just a glory road, but there are Gethsemanes, Via Dolorosas, Golgothas for us all.

And James fled before this new reality. The power, as he knew it, was dissipated. The shouted acclamations had turned to shrieks for blood. He was not prepared for this hot sweat of the death of dreams, for this gore and tearing flesh, for the earth groaning, the veil of unreality to be split in two.

Those of us who are involved in the work of the kingdom, on

whatever level, must beware of the Jamesian fiction, that spiritual power is equal to human success. We too must be willing to be broken; we must be willing to experience crucifixion, to taste the bitter memory of our own presumptuous words, and to choke on the ashes of the death of our unrealities.

And when we lay aside these fictions, what do we have? The same thing James had. Truth. The only reality that matters—Christ, the true source of power and authority.

They had gone back to their fishing after the cross. Perhaps they needed the money; and perhaps they sighed to themselves saying, "If only Jesus were with us, we wouldn't be doing this mundane, this humdrum thing."

But that was another fiction, one common to us all. We each sigh, "If only Christ were with us." And he is; he always is. He was standing on the shore, and he began again with them! He reenacted their first calling. "Cast the net on the right side of the boat!" he shouts from the shoreline. And they do with the same results.

It's exactly as though the Lord is saying to them, "Lesson one: Come follow me; but this time with inner eyes blasted wide, staring at truth, without powerful delusions, with no self-deceptions about your calling. Come follow me. And have I got a job for you to do!"

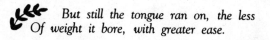 *But still the tongue ran on, the less*
Of weight it bore, with greater ease.

Samuel Butler

7

CUTTING AWAY THE DETRIMENTAL PAST

Sometimes, and for most of us, divine surgery is necessary to cut away the effects of the past.

Have you ever met anyone who got stuck in their childhood? Chronological age has gone ticking on toward mid-life, but these individuals still act, talk, and respond to life like they did when they were kids.

This is not a condition of mental retardation. We've all met and loved children who have become adults but whose biological set point refuses to allow the benefits of a fully harmonized maturity where mind, body, and spirit are in conjunction with each other. Nor is this childlikeness a case of maintaining enchanting innocence.

I've discovered that there are a lot of forty-five-year-old little kids walking around out there.

In a sense this kids-in-adults condition is almost as tragic as retardation because nothing physiologically prevents them from growing up; but for one reason or another, their maturity has been arrested somewhere in childhood. I am often distressed by meetings of old friends; conversation quickly reveals there is no more personal inner development than when we last met. Emotionally and psychologically regressed, their tongues quickly convey the fact that they are children charading as adults.

Mary Alice sat beside me in the dining hall of a large hotel. She was fifty-five years old at least, her hair was graying, and it wasn't too long before I felt like I was talking to Alice in Wonderland. At fifty-five she had a little girl's voice and smile, she had never married, and she kept talking about Daddy. Daddy did this and Daddy did that and Daddy was the most wonderful and spiritual of men.

The only problem was that Daddy had been dead for some twenty years.

Now strong fathers often imprint their children with their dominating and intriguing personalities. I have certainly been influenced profoundly by my own father. But Mary Alice found security in the memory of the relationship with her parent and had created a fantasy environment that shut out real life. Mary Alice had all the winsomeness and mannerisms of a twelve-year-old child ready to bloom into early womanhood with a voice of breathless wonder and eyes that glanced shyly.

I was discussing the phenomenon with a friend, and he said to me, "You know, my mother was a lot like that. She was the youngest of ten kids, and everyone treated her like the baby in the family. All the teachers in school had known her older brothers and sisters."

"But did she have these little girl mannerisms and this little girl tone of voice?"

"A little bit," answered my friend. "But the basic way she demonstrated that she was a little child was she kept expecting that everyone else would take care of her."

I've met adults like that too, walking around with the minds and outlook of children. In fact the writer John Marquand has done a wonderful job of portraying this type of personality in his book *Wickford Point*. The Brill family is doing a good job of living off the lingering reputation of an ancestor, the Wickford Sage, a New England poet of American historical renown who, nevertheless, was not a very good poet.

All of the characters in the Brill family are regressed children. Archie, the father, is a mural artist who never paints any murals. The young men are forever chasing after improbable jobs that won't amount to anything, and their sisters are forever chasing after rich, old family males who will never amount to anything. They are bound to each other with unhealthy dependencies, but it is their mother Clothilde who epitomizes the whole. She spends most of her life lounging on couches and asking, "Why doesn't anyone take care of me, darling? I get tired of doing everything for everybody. I have to take care of everyone else all the time. It would be nice if someone would take care of me for a change."

The problem is that everyone in the family says the same thing, each in his or her own way. Marquand has captured the tragedy of emotional children walking around in adult bodies by satirizing the eccentricities of the fictional Brill family.

Our tongue may be saying, "Why doesn't someone take care of me? Why doesn't anyone fix it, make it better, mend it, help me?" If it is, we better listen to its patter. Being adult means taking responsibility for our own life, not bending before the blowing wind of circumstances, assuming the privileges and terrors of personal autonomy, and seeing ourself primarily positioned to make life better for others.

"Oh-h-h-h-h, I wish someone would take care of me," our tongue sighs. We get mad when people don't do what in reality we are perfectly capable of doing for ourself. We're waiting for a mommy or daddy figure or an older brother-protector to come along and treat us like the baby of the family. Our regression is tragic, because in our case, we have the power to do something about our childishness.

We can begin to say to ourself, "Oh, grow up!"

I remember coming home from a twentieth high school class reunion and saying to my husband, "You know some of those people are not any older than they were in high school." Despite the fact that people often revert to yesteryear at such social functions and many considered least likely to succeed have made surprising strides, there were still incredible numbers who had just never grown up.

Nothing more wonderful had ever happened to some of them than the time they had been elected high school class president, cheerleader, homecoming queen, or had made first-string on the football team. That was the mountain of their maturity, but they had never struggled to climb higher. They had married and were raising children, but they were still teens of the fifties and sixties walking around in adult bodies during the last decades of the twentieth century.

When our tongue betrays that we are still a child in an adult body, major surgery is needed to remove the inner tumor.

What was that angry fit we threw yesterday? And why is this the habitual way we respond to stress or to frustration? We stamped and fussed and whined and shouted just like we used to when we were kids. That little scene was the equivalent of a grown-up temper tantrum. If a three-year-old had behaved so obnoxiously, some wise adult would have put him in his bedroom, closed the door, and walked away until he cooled down. Yet the child's behavior would have looked exactly the same as ours.

What is it our tongues talk about: Kid things. The things we bought. The clothes shopping we just did. What so and so said to so and so. Who was seen with whom. The gossip of the neighborhood. The trivialities of the street corner. Honestly now, have our ideas, our interests, or our spiritual conversations progressed any further than they were in our teen years?

The tongue is always a tattletale. It always tells on oneself.

Most of us discover at some point during our journey into maturity that our tongues speak volumes. In previous chapters we talked about the lumps on the inner person that needed to be removed because they were the source of certain forms of mouth disease; we have discussed surgeries minor and major. In this chapter we need to understand that some time or other, everyone needs to undergo further major operations of the soul in order to sever us from the detrimental influence of the child of the past on the adult of the present.

After reading David A. Seamand's book *Putting Away Childish Things*, I decided to hunt and see if there was any stunted child resident within me. I discovered some amazing residual childishness. The Mains family had been working together to accomplish an orderly and worshipful Sunday morning experience, but one of the major deterrents to achieving this goal was me. I got uptight whenever my family of six needed to leave our house and arrive at church.

I kept saying things on Sunday morning that I had no business saying, and I generally disturbed my family so much that we rarely arrived peacefully at church.

When I was really honest with myself and listened quietly to the Holy Spirit, I discovered I was still acting out an old pattern, a repetitive childhood experience.

Dad and Mom never left the house without this wild flurry of frantic disorder. Invariably someone couldn't find a shoe, the car keys, or their school books. Since I was the oldest child, responsibility for finding things always fell to me: "Karen Sue, see if you can find. . .run upstairs and look under the beds. . .go outside and check and see if we left it in the car. Karen Sue, help us get out of here on time." Due to this, I have developed an uncanny instinct for finding things; I can close my eyes and conjure up the hiding place of the lost thing, but in terms of leaving the house, I have been programmed to panic.

This insight into the child part of me, a holdover from the past hanging on with gripped fists, has helped me tremendously. In a sense, I have undergone a reconstructive surgical procedure. I have learned to recognize panic the moment it begins. I take deep breaths and remind myself that there is no reason for emotional anxiety, because we are not going to be late. If I'm ready, I sit quietly and wait for the rest of the family to get its act together. And I subdue my mouth. It does not need to give voice to the expressions that keep rising to my tongue, Hurry! Hurry! We'll be late! Are you ready?

Then I concentrate on calming the frantic little girl within. I tell her she doesn't have to panic, everything is under control, and we have plenty of time before arrival. If we arrive slightly late, it will not be a disaster. She doesn't have to worry anymore, everything is in my capable adult hands.

A silly example, perhaps, but most of our childish behavior is silly and aggravates those around us at home, at work, or at church.

I am also aware that people get stuck in their childhood because of trauma, the death or emotional distance of a parent, early childhood sexual abuse—a variety of terrible incidents can arrest adult development. In these severe cases, outside professional assistance is often needed to identify exactly the influence of the child within. This intervening help coupled with Scriptural insight can begin the healing process.

Upon approaching fifty-five, I do not want to be like the immature Mary Alice. I commend this major operation of divine therapeutic surgery—the cutting away of childishness.

What do we talk about? Do we talk about ideas? Are we eager to find friends who will discuss their spiritual journey? Do we spend more and more time in prayer? Do we extol God's presence? Express wonder at the created world? Speak words of wisdom, comfort, and life? Can we keep quiet? Are we bold in speaking when silence would be a sin? Do our tongues affirm, encourage, uphold fellow humans? Do they talk about growth, about becoming, about overcoming?

David has a friend who outwardly appears to be very humble. For a long while, we couldn't understand why we were generally annoyed after being around this personality. His effect on us was odd, like walking barefoot over sticky sugar spilled on the kitchen floor. Finally, David came home one evening and said, "You know, I just figured it out. I don't think I can stand any more of the subtle one-upmanship." Our friend was clever; he had functional humility, but he subtly dropped places, names, numbers, and invitations.

Sophisticated cover-ups are difficult to surgically remove because most of us attempt to hide our childishness from ourselves and from others. We have a whole psychological range of devices that shield us from looking truthfully within, many of which began in early life. But the tongue often reveals our ingenious hiding techniques.

We try to rid ourselves of traumatic experiences; and though other people allude to the incident, we have utterly no recall. This is called *repression.* Our tongue gives clues by not mentioning whole blocks of events and conversations. "I don't remember" often really means "I don't want to remember."

We have all heard the phrase, "the lady protests too much," meaning that someone is working too hard to be convincing and that the opposite of what is said is probably true. Our tongues can give clues by insisting with emotion that something didn't or couldn't happen. "He wouldn't be unfaithful to me! I know he would never do such a thing! It is absolutely beyond possibility! Don't talk about it! I don't want to hear!" The truth is that the woman has been wondering all along about so many late work nights, changes in attitude, and a coolness in communication. This is called *denial,* the refusal to accept things as they are, where the facts are realigned to establish the case we prefer.

We need to ask ourselves, Why am I protesting so much? Why do certain topics of conversation trigger emotional verbiage? What is within that I am acting out with my mouth?

In fact, we may often say exactly what is opposite to the truth. Denial, the realigning of truth, can become *reversal* in which "I don't love you" is changed to "I love you." Children who have been raised by parents whose actions were brutal, unloving, or uncaring but who said "You know I love you" have to contend with the fact of a childhood atmosphere of massive contradiction. One lie begets another, and that child often finds himself saying "I know my parents love me" when all evidence points to the opposite.

Have you ever gone through a harrowing experience and heard yourself say, "I feel okay. Numb, maybe. I don't have any emotional reaction to the event." This may be a case of *isolation*, focusing on the facts while blanking out the related reactions. The result is a bland version of experience. This is a habitual defense mechanism of my own. I am great in a crisis because I can isolate my emotional response from the actions that must be carried out at the moment, such as caring for a severed artery or answering the questions after an automobile accident. I learned years ago that I have a delayed response. I feel the full emotional impact several days after the traumatic event, and perhaps a double whammy, because I did not integrate my feelings with the actions as they happened.

The danger with isolation is when it becomes a habitual pattern rather than a coping mechanism for crisis. One wonders about a person who talks detachedly about traumatic, overwhelming events. These dispassionate words may simply be revealing an ability to dichotomize, to function intellectually without allowing room for messy, importunate emotions.

Rationalization is another protective technique. We don't

want people to know why we did what we did, or how. The little child within has not learned to take responsibility for its own behavior or to anticipate the natural outcome of certain types of actions. Rationalizations are slick lies that we tell not only to others but also to ourselves. It's the workaholic saying, "I can't stop working; I have so much to get done," when the truth is that he feels like he is losing control of life. He is mastered by having work to do; he doesn't know who he is apart from work; or he prefers work to spending time with family and friends. The rationalizations that our tongues can invent are endless; and we need to say to ourselves, "Oh, really? Is that exactly what happened? Is that truly why? Are we repeating the correct substance of the event?"

We humans are devious creatures, and we must come to terms with our inner selves—the influence of the child that needs to be cut away. We must understand our true and often horrifying motivations and intentions, the full weight of the world's evil that has fallen upon the past self that we now carry heavily into the present.

Our tongues speak the clues outwardly to what is going on inwardly. If the treasure chest of my heart is filled with toys—a floppy eared rabbit, a top, a picture book, a letter sweater, a class ring, the first jalopy, a diploma, or a small, brown-papered box of things too horrible to reveal—then my tongue will speak of them in one way or another; and this is the store from which I will draw when I need to give words to others.

Ephesians 4 teaches that we are no longer children, "tossed to and fro and carried about by every wind of doctrine. . .rather, speaking the truth in love, we are to grow up in every way into him, who is the head, into Christ" (vv. 14–15).

What is my tongue really saying? Do I need to grow up? I must begin this divine surgery and therapy. I must ask the Holy Spirit to show me the child within and ask him to give me a vision of the adult he truly wants me to be. And so must you.

Tongue Rehabilitations

There is no other joy than walking as He walked, and saying, loving, and doing that which he said, loved, and did.

William Law

8

REHABILITATION ONE
Tongue Exercises

The doorbell rings. Some unknown person stands outside and we have barely walked in the house only moments ago after having left early in the morning. The breakfast dishes are still piled in the kitchen sink, the newspapers are strewn over the coffee table, the pillows on the couch need fluffing, showing the indentations of teens' bodies. A mug half-full of cold coffee sits on the fireplace hearth and an empty bag of potato chips lounges forlornly in a favorite chair. The dining room table is piled with ongoing school projects, and none of the kids has carried his bucket of laundry the rest of the way upstairs to his room.

And there goes that bell again. Whoever is at the front door hasn't given up, but you don't feel like talking to anyone. All you want to do is take a hot bath, lie down for ten minutes and go to McDonald's for dinner. But the doorbell's still ringing, and at this point you have a multiple choice to make: (a) You can go down to the basement, back to the laundry room, turn on the washer and dryer, and legitimately say you didn't hear the doorbell ringing; (b) You can take a risk, open the front door, and hope it's the parcel post delivery man who'll leave the package and go away or (c) You can open the front door, find college friends you haven't seen in fifteen years, looking tanned, slim and successful and you can say to them, "Hey, its great to see you. Can you stay for dinner? We'll order Chinese food."

Life is punctuated with such minor dramas. My husband and I had a bright idea and traveled on Amtrak to and from California because we could take our two younger boys for the same price as our airfare. But after a week of speaking engagements, two days and two nights on the train, sleeping in the coach cars, we arrived home feeling unwashed and unrested. Furthermore, David and I caught colds, crossed the United States in a slightly feverish condition, blew our noses through two boxes of tissues, and infested our corner of the Superliner with positively virulent germs.

Pulling into the driveway of our home, we found a strange car parked outside and a man putting a note on the front door. "I listen to the broadcast and just happened to be in the area," he said. "I've read Karen's book on hospitality and knew it would be all right." By this time the dogs had been let out, leaping and barking, and the housesitter had arrived with mail and questions.

Believe me, I understand the dilemmas posed when the doorbell rings unexpectedly. All the multiple choices were flashing in my mind. I am not shielded against inhospitable attitudes just because I may have written a book on hospitality. So we stood in the driveway and talked to this gentleman, a nice man. But I wish now I had invited him in for a drink of something, lemonade or tea.

The ideal multiple choice answer is to extend a welcome, to give to any stranger or friend who comes into our lives a sense of greeting, a feeling that we are glad to see him or her, and that the possibilities in our meeting with one another are filled with unplumbed potential.

This is obviously a lesson I am still learning, and maybe the sick and weary welcome we gave under the homecoming confusion was the best we could give. I do know that every human being needs to feel that he or she is welcomed into the life of another, that there is someone, somewhere, who is glad because he or she has arrived, is near, has finally come. A welcome assuages the alienation of our common human dilemma, our cosmic loneliness. It makes the long night of life's existence bearable. Every human being from the tiniest infant to the oldest adult deserves welcome.

I think that *welcome* is one of the most Christ-like words we can speak to each other.

And yet, how rarely this happens. This word is shriveling because of disuse. How rarely do people stop in their busyness to greet one another, to chat on the block, to have a cup of coffee and talk about their days. How infrequently we inquire as to strangers' names, ask questions that indicate interest in their lives and families. How wonderfully rare it is when someone whispers, "I haven't seen you for so long, I missed you." How marvelous to hear, "You always make our times together special." We must learn to give to one another the words of welcome.

When a part of the body doesn't function properly, often rehabilitation will correct the problem or least improve it. Atrophied muscles can be brought to healthy activity again by the arduous rigor of exercise. We need to exercise our tongues, practice saying certain words over and over, so we will be able to correct serious dysfunction.

Are we ready? Let's repeat after me, "Welcome." Let's begin. "Welcome," (*two, three, four*). "Welcome," (*two, three, four*).

Take deep breaths and keep up to pace.

I'm so glad to see you," (*three, four*). "Wonderful to have you here," (*three, four*). "Won't you come along with us," (*three, four*).

"Welcome," (*one*). "Welcome," (*two*). "Welcome," (*three, and four*).

After the first therapy session, most people will be huffing and puffing. That's only normal. Most of us haven't said this word in a long time. Keep exercising. Pretty soon the frenulum, the tiny cord on the underside of the tongue that causes a condition known as *ankyloglossia* (or tongue-tiedness), will become limber and supple again. It will soon be saying welcome on its own.

Now while we rest awhile from these tongue exercises, let me explain why I chose the word welcome to begin rehabilitation.

Welcome is one of the words of life we can speak to each other. There are other words we could have practiced to begin this physical therapy session, words such as *I love you* or *You are beautiful to me*. *Thank you* is another excellent exercise word or *I forgive*, but *welcome* (in one of its forms; either through words or body language) is one of the first words we ever hear. It's the loving coo in a parent's voice, the unspoken light in a mother's eyes when she cradles her infant in her arms.

While attending a conference sponsored by professors at Duke University on the spiritual component as it relates to psychological and physical healing, I heard much informal discussion about prenatal trauma, about children who feel such rejection, even in their mother's womb, that they need help to become healthy adults. Someone ventured that perhaps this was one explanation for the struggles many adopted children experience in regard to insecurity or emotional maladjustment.

The truth is: Even the tiniest of infants suffers the effects of not being wanted or welcomed.

You can probably clearly remember when you were a little

child and your friends excluded you because "two is company; three is a crowd," and you were the third wheel. Hurt, you took yourself home where, hopefully, sympathetic parents dried your tears, held you, and explained that life is full of threesomes but that as long as the two of them lived, you would always be welcome.

Remember what it was like being on the outside group when you were a teen, with peers whispering and glancing your way, and the growing feeling of certainty that they were snickering about you? It's terrible to to be cut off from the group. Even now as an adult there may be moments when you wonder if anyone really wants you, cares about you, or will invite you to be with them.

This common human alienation is what makes the message of Scripture so incredible. Christ extends a welcome with his every word and action, "Come to me, all you who labor and are heavy laden, and I will give you rest" (Matt. 11:28). He understood how important it was for a little child to see a smiling, inviting face, to be welcomed by outstretched arms, and then to be invited to nestle close. "Let the children come unto me, and do not hinder them" (Matt. 19:14). There was no exclusion in Christ's welcome. He allowed the town whore (right before disapproving, self-righteous, religious dignitaries) to wash his feet with her tears and to wipe them dry with her hair. Such intimacy! But she was more important to him than the opinion of holy officialdom.

Christ allowed his days, plans, and agendas to be interrupted by intruding, exasperating, ill-timed, and demanding human need. Why? Because Christ knew that men's spirits were languishing for want of a welcome.

On the cross he offered a welcome to the thief hanging beside him. Christ extended an invitation, "Today, you will be with me in Paradise" (Luke 23:43). In our church, a chorus is often sung during the quiet when the congregation goes to the communion railing, "Oh, Lord, remember me/ when you come into your kingdom. Oh, Lord, remember me/ when you come into your kingdom." Christ's welcome is a welcome that remembers me. He will not forget my anguish, my sense of abandonment, my need to be with him. Nor will he forget yours.

Some have never felt welcomed in their entire lives. Some were never welcomed as infants, as children, as adolescents, or as adults. The world is full of people who need to know that though no one else welcomes them, Christ wants them near. He invites them to sit beside him at the banquet table of his love. His Spirit calls them by name when no one else phones, writes letters, sends invitations to social events.

Christ wants us. He stands as he did in the New Testament, with feet firm, hands outstretched, delight shining on his face, waiting for us to run into his embrace.

This is what a welcome is like, for those of us who choke when speaking the word, for those of us who have never really heard it spoken. It is what Christ spoke to the man with the withered hand, "Come here" (Mark 3:3). It is what he said to the tax collector in service to the infidel Romans who squeezed revenue from his fellow Jews, "Follow me" (Matt. 9:9). Welcome is Christ's hands laid on the leper's ulcerated flesh; he will not hesitate to touch the lesions on your soul. Christ is the Welcome.

Furthermore, his welcome is never a welcome that is withheld because of misbehavior. He may disdain our actions, our pettiness, our sinfulness, and particularly our arrogance and self-righteousness; but he will never withhold himself from any who comes crying out, "Forgive me, I am not worthy to be. . ."

James Dobson says the strong-willed child pops into the labor room shaking his fist and smoking a cigar. I agree. I had a child like that. We battled from day one. We battled over getting both in and out of high chairs, over putting bibs on and off, and over tying and untying gym shoes.

When this child went to school I had many interesting conversations with many teachers; we had a number of teachers over for dinner! A fourth grade teacher once called and said, "I'm having a little difficulty with your child. I've given all the children the assignment to study and make a report on a different country. Your child tells me he doesn't want to do this because he doesn't see how it will relate to his adult life."

One day I received a phone call and was informed that this child had been suspended for two days. We lived all of one-half block from the school building; and when thirty minutes had passed, I thought I'd better go looking for him. Standing on my front porch, I could see a little form bent dejectedly on the sidesteps by the playground—my son—and so I went to sit beside him.

Through the years, this child has taught me many lessons: he's taught me how to love, he's taught me that the parent's basic role is to help, not change, intensely driven personalities so they may grow whole and glorify their true Parent, God; he's taught me that when welcome is hardest to give, welcome is needed the most.

So I went and sat beside him and said, "I hear you've had a terrible, awful, horrible day."

I want all my children to know that no matter what they do, no matter how far they travel, no matter what they become, they will always be welcomed by me. Now, that does not mean I have to approve of all of their actions. David and I will never be party to the agreement that it is permissible to throw lit firecrackers into the hallways of grade schools—but that child, and all my children, no matter how they behave, are loved and wanted, often in spite of their humanity.

When we speak the words of welcome to one another, we are speaking the words of life. We are saying, "I welcome all of you.

I welcome the beauty of who you are. I welcome the struggle of what you are becoming. I welcome your idiosyncrasies as well as the petty irrationalities of you. I accept all of you. I welcome most of all the dream in you of what God wants you to be. I welcome the cross and the glory of your personality."

When we speak the words of life to one another, we speak the words of Christ. Our mouths become sacramental. Our tongues become his tongue in this weary, pain-filled world.

And in order to become proficient at speaking life, we must practice; we must rehabilitate these tongue-tied words. To whom can we speak welcome today? Is there a little child who needs to hear how proud we are to be his/her parent or friend? Is there a teen who needs to know he's loved. Is there a friend who needs to hear us say, "My friend"? What can we say to our spouse today that will be words of life? To a parent?

Now then: rested some from our first tongue exercise session? Let's do a little more. Once we become proficient, we can employ these exercises as aerobic maintenance, sharpeners, and toners. Let's open our mouths. Let's roll and loosen our tongues. Let's stretch those neck muscles. Ready? Repeat after me.

"Welcome," (two, three, four).

"Love to have you," (two, three, four).

"Sit beside me," (two, three, four).

"Come with us," (two, three, four).

"Welcome," (one); "welcome," (two); "welcome," (three and four).

Relax.

Of course, these exercises are strictly practice. They are tongue looseners, rehabilitation procedures that will help us overcome the debilities caused by mouth disease. The therapy is not considered successful until we put it into daily use and actually speak Christ to someone. That's when all the sweat and frustration of the physical therapy room pays off.

Rehabilitation for the tongue comes in varied forms; this therapy is one sample out of many. We can keep our tongues exercised by saying life-words; but to ensure as much improvement as possible, we must go on to rehabilitation two, three, and four.

No, 'tis slander,
Whose edge is sharper than the sword, whose tongue
Outvenoms all the worms of Nile, whose breath
Rides on the posting winds, and doth belie
All corners of the world.

Shakespeare
Cymbeline

9

REHABILITATION TWO
Confession

The wedding guests have gathered in great anticipation; the ceremony to be performed today has been long awaited. The orchestra begins to play an anthem, and the choir rises in proper order. The bridegroom and his attendants gather in front of the chancel. One little saint in the congregation, her flowered hat bobbing, leans to her companion and whispers, "Isn't he handsome?" The response is agreement, "Oh, my, yes. The handsomest."

One by one, the bridesmaids, heralds of the nuptials, begin to stride in measured footsteps. Several flower girls toss rose petals upon the white, unmarked aisle cloth. The sound of the organ rises, a joyous announcement that the bride is coming. Everyone stands and strains to catch a proper glimpse of the beauty—then a horrible gasp escapes from the congregation. This is a bride like no other.

In she stumbles—something terrible has happened. One leg is twisted; she limps pronouncedly. The wedding garment is tattered and muddy; great rents in the dress leave her scarcely modest. Black bruises can be seen welting her bare arms; the bride's nose is bloody. An eye is swollen, yellow and purple in discoloration. Patches of hair look as if they had actually been pulled from her scalp.

Fumbling over the keys, the organist begins again after his shocked pause. The attendants cast down their eyes. The congregation mourns silently. Surely the bridegroom deserves better than this! The handsome prince, who has kept himself faithful to love, should be joined in matrimony to the most beautiful of women—not this. His bride, the church, has been fighting again.

I am a child of the church. My earliest memories are filled with Sunday school classes, morning worship services, fellowship hours, youth groups, choir practices, evening evangelistic efforts, midweek prayer meetings, and summer Bible camps. I was raised in the church, and much of my adult life has been spent serving the church. I'm all too aware of church splits, minor fracases, nonamicable partings, and ecclesiastical skirmishes.

The church corporate, that household of the living God, has all too often formed itself into a series of fortified camps, entrenched not against the enemy without, but against the brotherhood within. Cold, silent wars or outright major offensives—it doesn't matter which; hostilities are occurring. Word bombardments are being unleashed. Slaughter is havocking the board meeting. Bloodshed is launched in the women's sewing circle. The bride is brawling again.

I'm all too aware that the tongue has had its deadly day and contributes greatly to the brawls the bride of Christ seems to be eternally waging. "Defend the doctrine!" is its battle cry. "Keep the faith pure! Protect the truth against liberalism! Guard the traditions against parochialism!"

James, the brother of Jesus, in writing his minor masterpiece on the tongue also responds to these verbal excuses we give for the fact that the bride of Christ is often little more than a scrappy street fighter. "What causes wars, and what causes fightings among you? Is it not your passions that are at war in your members?" (4:1).

Even more sadly, most of the conflicts in churches are over nothing more than matters of opinion (though we love to hide our immaturity behind high sounding theological phrases). The awful striving in the household of God stems mostly from the pitting of one's ideas against another's ideas. Rarely is there anything inherently moral involved in most of our choices; there is nothing right or wrong, nothing even smacking of doctrine. Most of our doctrinal disputes, if we would be honest, are due to personality conflicts.

And, oh, how the tongue, that little muscle, loves to set the bride brawling in the household of God!

How frequently the New Testament writers address this condition. Paul writes to Timothy, "Have nothing to do with stupid, senseless controversies; you know that they breed quarrels. . .The Lord's servant must not be quarrelsome but kindly to every one" (2 Tim. 2:23–24). "Avoid stupid controversies, genealogies, dissensions, and quarrels over the law, for they are unprofitable and futile" (Titus 3:9).

Again Paul writes to Timothy, "If any one teaches otherwise and does not agree with the sound words of our Lord Jesus Christ and the teaching which accords with godliness, he is puffed up with conceit, he knows nothing; he has a morbid craving for controversy and for disputes about words, which produce envy, dissension, slander, base suspicions, and wrangling among men who are depraved in mind and bereft of the truth" (1 Tim. 6:3–5).

Listen. The music march has begun; the great majestic chords are being struck. It is time for the marriage of the Lamb and the church. Your little congregation—the church you attend—is being caught up in the corporate catholic church. You are the bride of Christ about to take part in this remarkable love feast, this wonderful panoply of celebration. All the saints of the ages are waiting in hushed expectation for the sacred service to begin. Wait! Wait! Is the bride ready? Is her wedding dress in pristine shining order? Is she carrying a garland in her hands? Is her white lace veil catching the slight wind of the eternities?

Or will the hosts of heaven gasp when she makes her entrance? Will the bride look like she has just been brawling in the streets?

In the church there is one rehabilitation for this condition brought on by mouth disease. That is the practice of open confession. Let me repeat, because this rehabilitation is prescribed so infrequently that you might not have heard of the remedy. Brawling is the symptom of mouth disease and the rehabilitation is the practice of open confession.

How we love to overlook the little phrase from James 5:16, "Therefore confess your sins to one another." And the rule that seems to work best here is that open confession must be made in direct proportion to the circle of people we have offended or wronged.

If my tongue defames a brother publicly, true righteousness requires that I confess before everyone, "You know, I said the things I said because there is jealousy within my heart. Forget what I said, please, and pray for me that the Lord will heal my attitude."

This rarely happens, and the negligence of applying this medication is one of the reasons we have no spiritual power in our churches. It is one of the reasons we exist in a lukewarm Christian state, our prayers go unanswered, we do not affect our communities for good, and we turn the very stomach of the Almighty. There has never been a mighty moving of God in an

126

individual, in a local church, in a community, or in a nation without open confession being at work somewhere.

The tongue is a fire that destroys. In repentant, humble confession it can also be the instrument that allows for the sweeping flame of the Holy Spirit of God.

There is someone within the body of Christ whom I continually malign. I am aware that my tongue caused dissension in the board meeting. I spread gossip I knew to be damaging in that little fellowship circle. I turned the intercessory prayer cell into a criticism session. Quoting again from James, "My brethren, these things ought not to be so" (3:10).

I have been tearing the bride's veil, yanking at her hair, tripping her as she walks down the aisle, stomping on her when she falls, harrowing her with my words.

If I am ever going to have the spiritual life for which I long, if I am ever going to experience the love of the Apostolic church, I am going to have to make open confession.

Without the catharsis of confession the inward canister of my soul is not cleansed. It simply stores the poison and spills corroding acid whenever it is bumped or tipped. Amy Carmichal wrote in her little book *IF:* "If a sudden jar can cause me to speak an impatient, unloving word, then I know nothing of Calvary love. For a cup brimful of sweet water cannot spill even one drop of bitter water however suddenly jolted."

Confession purges the toxin, deodorizes the container, sterilizes it, readies it to hold the sweet, fragrant water it was intended to store.

One beautiful day God will change our inner selves, our outward bodies, and even our speech. Zephaniah 3:9 promises, "Yea, at that time I will change the speech of the people to a pure speech, that all of them may call on the name of the LORD and serve him with one accord." What a wonderful day that will be, but until that time we must do all we can to cure this disease of the mouth.

Let me make some very practical suggestions. In order to come to terms with our tongue's detrimental effect on the body of Christ, we need to undergo stern self-diagnosis. First, we must identify the area where the mouth has been a problem. Is there some Christian we continually defame? Who is that person? and how have we continually wronged him or her?

Now we must confess our lack of love. We must write this confession out on a piece of paper, in a prayer journal, or in a letter to a spiritual counselor we trust.

We must continue with the examination. Why do we have this problem toward this particular personality? What within us reacts so negatively? Are we jealous? Does that person have things that we don't have, a happy marriage, corporate success, wealth, a position in the church? Are we simply in disagreement with someone? Can we learn to allow opinion to remain opinion rather than personalizing it? Does this personality remind us of something within us we don't like? Are we projecting some of our own negative qualities onto someone else?

If we cannot put our animosity to rest, we need to go to someone who can act as a confessor, who will gently listen to our words; we need to kneel beside that person and speak aloud our confessions. The confessional, used in this sense as opposed to a routinized formality, has enormous powers to free us from our antagonisms.

Have we spoken against this person to one or two others? We must go to them and confess our bitterness, ask them not to repeat what we have said and then ask them to pray for us to find Christ's love. If the tongue has done such damage that it has acted like ink in water, diffusing the whole with murky color, then we need to apologize and make confession to the whole.

Perhaps we have maligned the pastor at every opportunity. We have not even made the effort to speak what is good about him. We need to make open confession. We need to write him a letter of apology and stand before the leadership of the church and say, "I have maligned the chosen human leader of this church in human rebellion. I need to ask and to receive this body's forgiveness."

Too hard? It is a terrible price to pay in terms of self-esteem; but without this confession in the church we will never know the residence of God's power among us.

Our tongues have done untoward damage. We need to make open confession. Is there a Bible study of which we are a part that meets regularly? We should speak the confession in this small group. "I have an area of hypocrisy in my life about which the Lord is dealing with me. I need to say, out loud, that I find myself pretending to be more spiritual than I am. I need your prayers to become truly the same within as I try to appear without."

There, that wasn't so hard was it? There's a sharing time in the church, and you confess that you have carried bitter feelings in your heart toward some of your brothers in the body. "I know God is displeased with my lack of love. I want to say out loud that I forgive and need forgiveness."

It is only when we speak so within the church today that the wedding march, which will one day ring in majesty, will begin now in our hearts. Confession is a cathartic rehabilitation that cleanses the inward sources of mouth diseases and allows the beautiful bride to begin her long walk toward that far distant altar.

"And so this is a conversazione, is it?" said that lady, speaking, as usual, not in a supressed voice. "Well, I declare, it's very nice. It means conversation, don't it, Mrs. Proudie?"

"Ha, ha, ha! Miss Dunstable, there is nobody like you, I declare."

"Well, but don't it? and tea and cake? and then, when we're tired of talking, we go away, isn't that it?"

"But you must not be tired for these three hours yet."

"Oh, I am never tired of talking; all the world knows that. . ."

Anthony Trollope
Framley Parsonage

10

REHABILITATION THREE
Silence

I bought my daughter a horse on her sixteenth birthday, and the family accused me of buying the horse as much for myself as for Melissa. They were right (I wanted one so much I had once lied for it!).

Lady Sundown, who stood sixteen-and-a-half hands high, was a lovely chestnut and white pinto, part quarter horse and part thoroughbred. She was spirited, but not unruly, and I loved to watch her arch her neck and lift her tail as we put her through her paces in the back pasture of the four acres where she was boarded—walking trot, running trot, canter, and gallop.

Without a doubt, owning this huge animal was a learning experience for me and for my children. We hung wide-eyed on the stable door and watched the practiced precision of the farrier as he shod her and sensed the confidence of the veterinarian as he examined her. We became amazingly casual about shoveling manure, loading heavy bags of grain, and hauling hay in the station wagon.

One of the most beautiful things about owning Lady Sundown was the great confidence and discipline I saw developing in my teenage daughter. There is something about being responsible for a large animal. It must be fed twice a day and watered; the stalls must be clean. After a while the horse knows that you are its owner and whinnies a greeting when you drive into the driveway and park by the stable.

The horse becomes amazingly sensitive to your desires. She reads the meaning of your body motion in the saddle; and you sense when she is flighty, ready to shy. You know she dips her head before moving into a canter, "Whoa, baby; take it easy, baby." "Easy, easy, now Lady," you find yourself saying. And the animal understands, and you feel you have become one lovely unit of motion, horse and rider, in sync, together a rhythm of pounding hoof and creaking saddle.

But I was reminded of perhaps the greatest lesson of all when I finally developed the confidence to take Lady Sundown on my first solo gallop. As I raced her at full speed (surprisingly smooth) with her long legs pounding beneath me and her head stretching out before me and with the sound of each row of corn in the cornfield going *phyt-phyt-phyt-phyt-phyt* in my ears, I suddenly thought of the words from the book of James.

"For we all make many mistakes," he wrote. "And if anyone makes no mistakes in what he says, he is a perfect man, able to bridle the whole body also. If we put bits into the mouths of horses that they may obey us, we guide their whole bodies" (James 3:2–3). So true, all sixteen-and-a-half-hands high of it! Being able to control Lady Sundown with a mouth metal, English reins, and a thin chin strap gave me an enormous sense of satisfaction. To be in working harmony with the huge bulk of that animal was something hard to describe.

Even more satisfying is learning to curb the tongue, wearing a bridle and bit on the mouth so to speak. Through the years, after struggling mightily with my chronic case of mouth disease, I have discovered that one of the most effective rehabilitations for the tongue is the bridle of silence. And it is only through the regular practice of silence that we can learn to refrain our mouths from speaking; or better yet, through silence we learn when to speak and when not to speak.

In *Celebration of Discipline*, Richard Foster addresses this issue:

> The disciplined person is the person who can do what needs to be done when it needs to be done. The mark of a championship basketball team is a team that can score points when they are needed. Most of us can get the ball in the hoop eventually but we can't do it when it's needed. Likewise, a person who is under the Discipline of silence is a person who can say what needs to be said when it needs to be said. If we are silent when we should speak, we are not living in the Discipline of silence. If we speak when we should be silent, we again miss the mark.

"He that knows not how to hold his tongue, knows not how to talk," says Thomas Fuller. The apostle James maintains that we are perfect people when our tongues are under control. The tongue is a thermometer of our spiritual condition but it also acts as a thermostat. Proverbs praises this ability to control the tongue:

"When words are many, transgression is not lacking, but he who restrains his lips is prudent" (10:19).

"He who goes about as a talebearer reveals secrets, but he who is trustworthy in spirit keeps a thing hidden" (11:13).

"Even a fool who keeps silent is considered wise; when he closes his lips, he is deemed intelligent" (17:28).

All of these Scriptures produce resonance in my soul. I am longing to better develop the great discipline of silence. Scriptural silence is always inner attentiveness. Though silence sometimes involves the absence of speech it always sets the stage for listening. Bonhoeffer wrote, "Real silence, real stillness, really holding one's tongue comes only as the sober consequence of spiritual stillness." Simply to refrain from talking, without a heart listening to God, is not silence. Catherine de Hueck Doherty has written, "All in me is silent and. . .I am immersed in the silence of God."

It is only out of developing the discipline of spiritual silence, out of this act of constant inward attentiveness toward God that we can learn to fully control our tongues.

When Lady Sundown was in the stall, waiting to be groomed for riding, I developed a nervousness as to whether or not I would really be able to get that bridle with all its straps and chains and rings and buckles on her head. Melissa learned to do this with amazing ease, but I had trouble because for me the horse often refused to take the bit, shoving it out of her mouth with her tongue or by shaking her head. She knew I was nervous and took advantage of me, and much time was wasted in the stable getting that contraption on the horse.

For the Christian, consciously developing the discipline of silence is comparable to a horse "taking the bit." We deliberately allow our tongues to be controlled by the heavy metal piece of quiet.

How remarkably Christ demonstrated this control in John 8. "The scribes and the Pharisees brought a woman who had been caught in adultery, and placing her in the midst they said to him, 'Teacher, this woman has been caught in the act of adultery. Now in the law Moses commanded us to stone such. What do you say about her?' This they said to test him, that they might have some charge to bring against him" (vv. 3–6).

Christ answered them with silence. He bent down and wrote with his finger on the ground. Then finally, from the power of that stillness he spoke, " 'Let him who is without sin among you be the first to throw a stone at her' " (v. 7). Then he bent his head again and withdrew into silence until only the woman was left standing before him.

Isaiah's messianic prophesy testified to the future power of this silence, "He was oppressed, and he was afflicted, yet he opened not his mouth; like a lamb that is led to the slaughter, and like a sheep that before its shearers is dumb, so he opened not his mouth" (Isa. 53:7).

And so it came to pass, the Word that was in the beginning, now within the enfolding drama of redemption becomes dumb, making no statement in his own behalf: "But Jesus made no further answer, so that Pilate wondered" (Mark 15:5). "When Herod saw Jesus, he was very glad, for he had long desired to see him, because he had heard about him, and he was hoping to see some sign done by him. So he questioned him at some length; but he made no answer" (Luke 23:8–9).

Without knowing it, Herod was witnessing a sign of Christ's power; he was beholding a demonstration of the majestic display of silence, a perfect man having himself under control.

I have great need for silence. Often when I begin a major writing project or have to speed up one that is going slowly, I go away for an uninterrupted week of work. These times have proven beneficial, not only in terms of starting and finishing projects, but as heightened spiritual growth accelerators. Last year I spent a week alone in a cabin in California setting the time aside for prayer, fasting, and contemplation. It turned into what I can only describe as a spiritual honeymoon! The Lord made his presence extremely close to me and assured me of his love.

A friend met me at the airport and loaned me her recording of John Michael Talbot's *For The Bride.* One song, "The Canticle of the Bride," set the motif for my seven days before the Lord.

Let us kiss with the touch of our life.
Call me Lord to your chamber,
For your kiss is an excellent wine
Flowing smoothly poured out for another.
For the bride belongs to the Lover

And the Bridegroom yearns for His bride.
So come to the night, there to empty our life
To be fulfilled with the flowers of dawn.

All the Scriptures I read, all the meditations of my heart, even my dreams centered on the truth: God is the lover of our souls, and he wants us to give ourselves to him in absolute fidelity. Song of Solomon says, "Set me as a seal upon your heart, as a seal upon your arm; for love is as strong as death, jealousy is as cruel as the grave. Its flashes are flashes of fire, a most vehement flame. Many waters cannot quench love, neither can floods drown it" (8:6–7).

I had not gone seeking God's love but to set myself aside in silence before him. I wanted time for uninterrupted Bible study, for prayer, for gathering the initial thoughts for a major creative work; but his purpose for the retreat was to personalize the communal promises made to the nation of Israel through the prophet Hosea: "I will betroth you to me forever. . .and you shall know the LORD" (2:19–20). "And in that day, says the LORD, you will call me, 'My husband'" (2:16).

Ever since that special week, I have attempted to schedule regular retreats of silence. I go away by myself to a quiet place and for twenty-four hours I allow the Lord through prayer to commune with me. I particularly try to have a day set aside before the holy seasons, such as Nativity and Lent. And I find that the more I develop my capacity to refrain from speaking and carry silence in my soul, the better guard I have over my tongue.

In the past I would have loved to testify about God communing with me, but now after years of seeking silence, I find a reluctance to share from my cherished privacy about my own individual spiritual walk. I consider this reluctance a healthy growth indicator, and I only mention it in my writing as an encouragement to others.

Foster gives extremely practical suggestions as to how to begin this discipline. "The first thing we can do," he writes, "is to take advantage of the 'little solitudes' that fill our day. Consider the solitude of early morning moments in bed before the family awakens. Think of the solitude of the early morning cup of coffee. There can be little moments of rest and refreshment when we turn a corner and see a flower or a tree."

The next suggestion he makes is to find a "quiet place," such as a closet, a storage room, or a kneeling bench before a window, and use it as a place to pray, read, and think. I find that a walk of three and one-quarter miles takes me a little over an hour to complete; this sometimes becomes my mobile quiet place. I leave the distractions and demands of family and home and meet with God as I'm on the go, returning both restored and exercised!

The third suggestion by Richard Foster is to discipline ourselves so that our words are few and full. This is a hard discipline for me.

I have to deliberately choose not to speak but to ask questions and then listen. I have to enforce upon myself a rule of not talking about where I have traveled, what I have done, whom I have met, or the brilliance of my children. I've learned that there are many things I know that I don't have to tell.

I am working on not interrupting people. This is a terrible habit, this rushing in to complete their sentences. If they pause but for a moment, to choose a word, I finish their thoughts. This intrusion negates the meaning of someone else's ideas, their individual thinking apparatus; and it erupts mostly at the times when I have not been nurturing silence.

On a weekly level, I must have at least an hour for prayer

each day, one morning a week to sit before the Lord and listen, regular enough getaway times, and days alone preceding or following retreats at which I minister.

Wayne E. Oates in his book *Nurturing Silence in a Noisy Heart* writes, "Silence is a discipline of choosing what to say and what to listen to. Nurturing silence then, is the growth of the power of discernment as to what will be the focus of our attention, care, and commitment." I cannot direct my life without habitual quiet.

And as for tongue control, silence is Rehabilitation Treatment Number 3. Plutarch in *Rules for Preservation of Health* wrote, "Remember what Simonides said, — that he never repented that he had held his tongue, but often that he had spoken."

When Melissa went off to college, the painful responsibility of selling the horse fell on me. I felt like I was auctioning a child, but the deed, after much emotional vacillating, was done; and, very frankly, I still miss my riding day.

Always a novice rider, I fumble with the reins, the bridle, and the bit. Fingers spread, I force metal into the wet mouth. My right hand pulls the browband over the forelock and the headpiece over the ears. I buckle the throatlatch. If I drop the cloth halter on the horse's neck too soon, Lady Sundown might bolt into the barnyard, and I will have to plod through the mud from recent rains to coax her back into the barn.

Finally, I tighten the girth. The horse lets out the breath she has been holding. I tighten it again. Then out of the paddock onto the lane. Lower the left stirrup. One notch above twelve. Heels down, head up, back straight. Reins in both hands, gloved now. A hard ride worries raw the skin on my fourth finger. Walk the first mile. Post up. Post up. Down into the alfalfa field. Post. Post. Cross the creek. Past the gardens, the farmer waves. Onto the macadam, now into the cornfield. *Now* go, *Lady*, go! Again, the corn rows sound *phyt-phyt-phyt-phyt-phyt* in my ear. *That's good, Lady! That's good!*

Behold! With what a small bit the huge animal is tamed.

A despot doesn't fear eloquent writers preaching freedom—he fears a drunken poet who may crack a joke that will take hold.

E. B. White
One Man's Meat

11

REHABILITATION FOUR
Laughter

All of us face times when we wonder if we will ever laugh again. These are the dreadful grinding, sandpaper days that stretch on and on, abrading sensitive, half-healed wounds, filing away at the tissue of the mind; wearying eternities that buffet us with the attrition of pain, grief, despair, illness, or loss.

I have known these moments and wondered where laughter had gone, only to discover that laughter cloaks itself in disguise and springs out from its hiding place to surprise us when we are most garroted with the enormity of life; it shouts, *Olly, Olly, oxen free!* It invites us to rush to life's game again, to cast aside for a moment the weights of labor and responsibility, and to roll down the greening hillside, over and over, tumbling faster, bumping, plummeting, strangling for air between chortled shouts and gasps.

Laughter is God's good friend.

Not only does laughter lift us emotionally and psychologically, numerous studies have proven that laughter works enormous physical benefits. Patricia Keith-Spiegel, a researcher, summarized the work of many by concluding, "Laughter and humor have been hailed as 'good for the body' because they restore homeostasis, stabilize blood pressure, oxygenate the blood, massage the vital organs, stimulate circulation, facilitate digestion, relax the system, and produce a feeling of well being."

No wonder we feel better after a good laugh.

Dr. William Fry, a Stanford University researcher, has written:

> Humor minimizes the intensities of both fear and anger. . .Laughter has many of the same benefits as exercise. Both provide increased heart rate, blood pressure and circulation, as well as increased frequency and depth of respiration, with expulsion and replacement of residual air in the lungs and coughing out of mucus accumulations. Both provide musculoskeletal activity and a sense of well-being and pain relief, possibly attributable to increased levels of endorphins, the body's natural opiates. Indeed, laughter can be said to give the body a mini-workout that has been compared to stationary jogging.

The physical benefits of humor are so well known that many hospitals and clinics offer classes in "humor as a stress reliever." The Ravenswood Hospital in Chicago created an ambitious self-help program that now offers support to those undergoing inordinate stress: epileptics, parents in distress, family members of the disabled, victims of crime, survivors of incest, single parents, widows and widowers, and children who care for aging parents. Laughter, or being able to laugh again, has an enormous placebo effect and alleviates the sharp edge of anxiety and grief.

Norman Cousins writes in *Anatomy of an Illness* about his personal battle against a rare, arthritic-like disease about which the doctors gave him no hope for cure. Analyzing his condition from an informed layperson's perspective, he decided to take the responsibility for his body into his own hands. In consultation with his sympathetic physician, he ended his medical treatments, substituting controlled doses of ascorbic acid; then he submitted himself to delightful humor therapy. Moving from a hospital that he felt was not conducive to the restful atmosphere he needed, he relocated himself in a nearby hotel room, hired a nurse, rented a projector and comedy films, and began to make a joyous discovery:

> Ten minutes of genuine belly laughter had an anesthetic effect and would give me at least two hours of pain-free sleep. When the pain-killing effect of the laughter wore off, we would switch on the motion-picture projector again, and not infrequently, it would lead to another pain-free sleep interval. Sometimes the nurse would read to me out of a trove of humor books.

Despite the diagnosis that his condition was degenerative, each day Cousins' sedimentation rate, which had been alarmingly elevated, was reduced until he was able to return to work and resume a normal lifestyle. He continued to improve in his physical strength and the symptoms of disease decreased.

"A cheerful heart is a good medicine," says Proverbs (17:22). Whenever I find that the responsibilities of ministry and home and personal growth have become overwhelming, I plan for an evening of laughter. A funny story around the dinner table, deliberately looking for the comic side of life, then taking time to develop the preposterous potentials of the recent funny event, telling the incident to someone, laughing together—these all alleviate the destructive quality of living too much on the edge.

Mark Twain, American humorist, wrote in *Tom Sawyer* that an "old man laughed loud and joyously, shook up the details of his anatomy from head to foot, and ended by saying that such a laugh was money in a man's pocket, because it cut down the doctor's bills like everything."

When I get achy from stress, the muscles across my neck knot because of tension. Instead of thinking that I need a hot bath (though it is wonderfully relaxing in itself), I find myself longing for a good laugh.

Laughter has a wonderful way of reducing social stiffness. Recently, David and I were given the responsibility of moderating a group of five couples, pastors and wives. We began the evening by stating that we knew from personal experience how the ministry was filled with the drama of life, its good times and its bad times. What we wanted them to do was to discuss as couples two pastoral incidents, one tragic and one comic, and then share them with the group.

The couples took ten minutes to choose two incidents. David and I could hear comments that would slip out from beneath the mumble of discussions, "Oh, I couldn't share that; it's too embarrassing!" Later the twosomes began to laugh as they recalled some funny experiences.

A wife started by sharing a truly funny story about her husband and we laughed; another told a wild, riotous, unbelievable tale. We laughed together for two hours and the stories kept getting funnier and funnier. We wiped the tears from our eyes; we gasped for breath. "I wasn't going to share this," said one pastor. "In fact, I haven't told this to anyone because it's the kind of story people who aren't in the ministry wouldn't understand but. . ." and he revealed his hilarious episode.

Looking back on that evening, I can't think of a quicker way to introduce relaxation, camaraderie, joy, feelings of fellowship, and ease to a group of people who don't know one another. Laughter is the all-time best icebreaker.

Obviously, humor is one of the ways we can bring words of

life into the world; it is a God-given means to bring health to our own bodies.

Yet humor also has its detrimental side. We need to be careful about the jabs, the painful darts, the slicing thrusts, the clever repartee that kills the spirit, humiliates, quashes the liveliness in another.

In the book *Traits of a Healthy Family*, the author Dolores Curran lists one trait as: "The healthy family has a sense of play and humor." Mrs. Curran composed her list from responses to a survey given to over five hundred family professionals— teachers, doctors, pastors, social workers, psychologists.

> A sense of humor in the family also keeps things in perspective and works as an antidote to drudgery, depression, and conflict within families. Members of families that have a sense of humor can say to themselves, "I am not the center of the universe or even of this family. This situation I'm in is not going to change my life. I can laugh about it." Members who have this distance on themselves help defuse potentially explosive family situations.

Then the author goes on to say that these healthy families use humor positively, defusing anger, perhaps reiterating a quip made by a child earlier in his life that will in the present alleviate tension and stress. Once when one of our children was small and had been misbehaving, he found himself at the end of a stern parental lecture. "What are we going to do?" asked the adult. In self-resignation the child suggested, "Why don' we jes' frow me ina garbage." That has become the signature statement for any time in our family when one member is frustrated with himself, "jes' frow me ina garbage I guess."

But then Mrs. Curran points out the destructive potential of humor as well. Members of healthy families tend to laugh *with* each other while members of unhealthy families tend to laugh *at* each other. Humor based on ridicule is devastating in its results;

wise parents realize that personal shortcomings are not material for family jests.

Healthy families recognize and reject turnoff words and put-down phrases. Comments made in jest may in reality be insults to some. For instance, I cannot bear to be teased about not being able to balance my checkbook; this is indeed a sensitive issue and my family has learned to walk warily around the topic. I can tell jokes about *my* inability, but woe be to the humorist who presumes on this forbidden territory himself.

The same is true in the social groups that are not necessarily family. We can use humor positively or we can use it destructively. I have a jugular vein instinct; I can intuitively strike at someone's tender area, and through the years, the Holy Spirit has had to discipline me about the negative potential in my humorous tongue. Some of the funny things I say are not funny—even though people are laughing. Consequently, I attempt to tell funny stories about myself, to tell the crazy things that have happened to me, and to laugh at my own ridiculous propensities.

David and I meet monthly with a small group. Last year several of the couples were going through traumas: job pressures, terminal diseases, the questions of healing and faith, the loads of ministry organizations with their constant financial need. Sensing that all of our spirits were weighted with concern, I invited the group to bring one piece of reading material that was humorous or to bring one story out of their own past that was funny. And they did. We started with the penny game that my children play when their friends come to our house. Each player is given ten pennies. The starter says, "I have never done such and such" (gone skinny dipping for instance) and throws his penny on the coffee table. All those who have never done the same thing toss their coins, which means that all those left are exposed (pardon my bad pun!).

Laughter begins. "I have never made my bed everyday for a whole week." "I have never been to London."

Then we began to read our stories and tell our tales. Riotous, exuberant laughter came shouting into my living room. Our sides ached; we had to stand to get our breath.

David told his "First Baptism" story.

We had begun a church in the heart of the inner city of Chicago in 1967 and we met in Teamster's Union Hall, Local 705, which consisted of a ballroom, a barroom, ladies' and men's rooms but no baptismal tank. There were many new converts; so, consequently, we borrowed an auditorium from a Japanese church on the north side of the city. That church was newly built; and since they hadn't as yet had a baptism, we thought it very generous of them to loan us their facilities.

David was exceedingly nervous and absolutely unconvinced about the buoyancy of water, so he did some practice dry runs on me in the living room of our home to prepare himself for the awesome first baptism—"In the name of the Father" (practice dunk), "the Son" (practice dunk), "and the Holy Spirit" (practice dunk).

The eventful evening arrived, a cold winter night; and the church gathered. In a borrowed baptismal robe, David entered the waters only to discover that someone had turned on the tap and let it run, emptying into the tank icy cold unheated water. In the most dignified way possible (while he danced hopefully unobtrusively from foot to foot), he lowered the first candidate, a tall and athletic young woman, beneath the surface of the tank. If he had ever doubted for one moment whether he would be able to lift her out of the baptistry, his doubts were dispelled; because as soon as she hit the waters, she immediately, even forcefully, surfaced.

Unbeknownst to my husband, the drama was just unfolding.

The young woman, in her clinging baptistry robe, *splooshed, splooshed, splooshed* to a right exit doorway only to open it and find the chill, winter Chicago wind blowing and the snow flurrying. It was an exit all right. Not to be outdone, she *splooshed, splooshed, splooshed* across the platform to another door, opened it—a broom closet. At this point David had the congregation bow their heads in prayer, but not much prayer went on because we could hear the first candidate *sploosh, sploosh, sploosh, sploosh, splooshing* down the long center aisle.

The second candidate for baptism was an international student whom one of our staff had led to the Lord. He had been converted while hospitalized for kidney failure; and the Lord had not only touched his soul, but also his body had been cured as well. He entered the water and gave a testimony (a long testimony) to a miraculous work of God—while David (as unobtrusively as possible) danced from frozen foot to frozen foot.

When it came time to immerse the young man, David, concerned about his own impending hypothermia, misjudged the distance and conked the new convert's head on the stairs that led into the tank. Crash! Splash! But the water was so cold it had instant revivifying effects and David was convinced the international student could now give testimony to *two* miraculous healings!

The *sploosh, sploosh, sploosh* scenario had to be replayed, and we in the congregation bowed our heads as before, listening through our prayers to the second damp exit, *sploosh, sploosh, sploosh, sploosh, sploosh.*

Laughter, what a gift from God!

Conrad Hyers has written in *The Comic Vision and the Christian Faith,* "Insofar as we remember our humanity, the play of humor is not irreverent or irresponsible but a moral and spiritual necessity. Without humor we become something less, not more, than human. We become not more divine but more demonic."

When I look at my life, when I see the intimate way he works with me, I'm convinced God has a sense of humor as well. How often, in the midst of some struggling growth, I suspect that divine grin is turned my way. I know one of the reasons he loves me is because I have given him so much laughter.

If my tongue is feeling the effects of illness, I must find a reason for healthy laughter. What a wonderful rehabilitation treatment! Laughter brings instant relief, gives a new view on life, exercises the internal vital organs, and frees me from the stresses and tensions that cause me to misspeak myself.

Wit has aroused deep interest in a considerable number of people of letters, philosophers, psychologists, psychiatrists, and neurologists. Often it has been studied as a form of art, at times as a psychological process, and occasionally as a special expression of the spirituality of man (some of the holiest people I know demonstrate an incredible quality of joy). Understanding the makeup of humor is a complicated and still ill-defined process.

Nevertheless, at its very basic level, good laughter is one of the rehabilitations for mouth disease.

Raymond A. Moody, Jr., writes in his book *Laugh After Laugh* about the benefits of laughter. After giving a presentation on the topic, he tells of a professional comedian who came up to him and said that on those occasions on which he had really made his audience laugh, he had always told his wife, "I killed them tonight!" Now, he said, he was going to tell her, "I helped them live!"

Let us learn to give to one another the living gift of laughter.

Healthy Measurements

And the multitudes asked him, "What then shall we do?" And he answered them. . .

Luke 3:10

12

SPEAKING WORDS OF LIFE TO GOD

Words—how beautiful they are; how they roll on the tongue and evoke visions in the mind. How they call forth emotion, and what a wonderful gift words are to man. Bulwer-Lytton said, "The magic of the tongue is the most dangerous of all spells." Read another poem by Edna St. Vincent Millay, "Counting-out Rhyme."

> Silver bark of beech, and sallow
> Bark of yellow birch and yellow
> Twig of willow.
>
> Stripe of green in moosewood maple,
> Colour seen in leaf of apple,
> Bark of popple.
>
> Wood of popple pale as moonbeam,
> Wood of oak for yoke and barn-beam,
> Wood of hornbeam.
>
> Silver bark of beech, and hollow
> Stem of elder, tall and yellow
> Twig of willow.

Words are wonderful, but how awful, how utterly void, nullified, vacant we would be without words.

While teaching at a writer's conference, I met a young woman who suffered from a severe case of cerebral palsy. I actually heard her before I met her. Her cry, her vocalization, sound wrenched gutterally from her throat, was impossible to ignore. Riding twisted in her wheelchair, her head bobbed, her mouth hung open, and her hands jerked. "This is Sally," someone explained by way of introduction. "Sally hears your broadcast and wanted to meet you."

"Uh-huh-h-h-h-h-h," said Sally.

We talked, or rather I asked questions while Sally arduously poked out the answers, letter by letter, struggling to point a finger at the keyboard on a computer-like attachment. I spent most of that fellowship break getting to know Sally; it would have taken a heart of stone not to be overwhelmed by the courage of this woman to attend a conference about words, their usage, their combinations, and their publication with so little facility for verbal command herself.

Sally gave me some of the things she had written. The stories and thoughts revealed childhood abandonment to cold institutionalization, snatches of glimpses about God's redemptive love reaching her, and a determination to become something beyond predictions. One little essay was about children who laughed at her condition; I was impressed by its lack of rancor, bitterness, or pain. She understood that their laughter was because of incongruity, not because of unkindness; the piece ended by saying that she would have laughed also in such a situation.

I have thought about Sally (and others like Sally) many times as I use words; for Sally to express herself took infinite endurance. I attempt to never take this ability for granted.

My father lost his use of language because of encephalitis that scrambled the signal systems of his brain. We watched him die slowly for four long years after the initial illness. At first, the speech therapist would visit him several times daily to encourage his language facility. These were painful sessions because my father was unable to imitate even the simplest sounds that a six-month-old infant would be able to repeat. After awhile there was nothing more to be done and we transferred my father from the rehabilitation hospital to a nursing home where he slowly declined, losing more and more language ability until he finally ceased to use words of any kind.

During those years I had much time to think about the loss of language, of being without words, or being without the right words. Despite my father's aphasia (language loss), we communicated as best we could within the circumference of diminishing rationality.

We all have a Father with whom we have a language problem; yet in this case, it is not he who has the language loss. It is his children who are impaired. Oh, they can speak of everything else. They can talk of baseball and something the hairdresser did. They can talk about their children being potty trained or about their own aches and pains. They can complain about black spot on roses or speculate with dread about the coming nuclear holocaust. They can talk about leisure activities and buying new cars and building new homes, but they have no facility at spiritual linguistics.

They cannot speak the words of faith or whisper a morning prayer. They cannot say, "I love; I adore; I extol." They cannot, like a little child crawling into its father's lap, say in so many ways, "You are the bestest, nicest, most wonderfulest Daddy in the whole wide world!"

I know what it's like to love someone who is without language, to wait long afternoons as the sun grows thick, then thin toward dusk, and to hope for one word to slip through the confused infrastructure of the inner brain, familiarly spoken, sounding like the old days, with the melodious accents of love and delight. I know what it is like: it's tearing; it's grievous; it hurts.

How awful it must be to be God with a world full of children who have no language for him.

Lord, how do you stand this silence, this great vacuum of universal subtraction, this negation, this vast glass bell that never rings, never sounds your praises?

Unlike my father, God has never forgotten my name and yet hours pass without me remembering his. Let us all pray that we will be cured from our spiritual aphasia and will begin to speak the language of love to God. These tongues are gifts; these words are tools. The mouth is intimately linked to the human heart and mind, but we rarely use them for their highest purpose.

"Rejoice always," writes Paul. "Pray constantly, give thanks in all circumstances" (1 Thess. 5:17–18). "Rejoice in the Lord always; again I will say, Rejoice" (Phil. 4:4). "Be filled with the Spirit, addressing one another in psalms and hymns and spiritual songs, singing and making melody to the Lord with all your heart, always and for everything giving thanks in the name of our Lord Jesus Christ to God the Father" (Eph. 5:18–20).

Again, our tongues tell; if we never speak of spiritual things, can't we safely assume spirituality holds no priority for us?

Man's sin gene has destroyed his ability to speak the language of heaven. In a sense, the church is the rehabilitation center here on earth that enables us to practice the words we have lost. But unless we practice, unless we struggle to repeat praise, adoration, and testimony, how will we take our place beside that great verbal multitude who have been practicing for centuries, and how will we bow our knees along with every other knee and loosen our tongues and proclaim that Jesus is Lord?

The following questions can be used for self-evaluation to determine the severity of our spiritual aphasia.

1. On an average, how often in the day do I speak about God's work or his love in my life?

2. Do my first thoughts in the morning, those thoughts that form words, leap in love toward a heavenly parent who is waiting to hear me speak?

3. When I have leisurely conversational moments with friends, how often do I speak of spiritual matters?

4. Do I feel comfortable talking about God, Christ, and the Holy Spirit? Or do I choke?

5. Can I speak to my children, to my spouse, to my best friend about a recent incident in which I learned something more about God?

6. Are there phrases from hymns, snatches of Scripture, thoughts from a sermon that keep repeating themselves in my heart?

7. Do I love saying over and over the many names of God— Jehovah-Jireh, Emmanuel, His Majesty, my Lord and my God?

If we answer no to most or to all of these questions, my diagnosis is that we have a moderate to severe case of spiritual aphasia, a language disorder of our spirits, and we need to deliberately commit ourselves to linguistic rehabilitation.

Traditionally, the means to determine whether one is a Christian or not has always been twofold: First, we must believe in our hearts; second, we must confess with our mouths that Jesus Christ is the Christ; then we shall be saved. Verbal confession is always considered the concrete evidence of spiritual conversion.

Perhaps an initial test of language health is positive confession, even if we only begin by saying it to ourselves. *The Lord, he is the Christ. The Lord, he is the Christ. The Lord, he is the Christ.* Speaking words of life to or about God is not really very difficult; it is simply doing what we already know to do.

Southern writer Flannery O'Connor possessed a remarkable skill for poking holes in human pretensions. In her short story

"The Enduring Chill," she wrote about Asbury, a young man who moved to New York to become a writer. His tremendous aspirations about his artistic ability are unceremoniously deflated by his sister Mary George who unkindly points out that he has never written anything.

Eventually Asbury returns home to the farm with a mysterious disorder. Mary George thinks it's psychosomatic, and his mother thinks he's having a nervous breakdown. Actually, Asbury is filled with intellectual hauteur. He considers himself superior in every way to the family and country folk around him. And he thinks he is dying.

The truth is that in a pique he drank unpasteurized milk from his mother's dairy and is now suffering from undulant fever, a condition, according to the country doctor, that will "come and go, but won't kill him."

In the middle of all this, Flannery O'Connor brings a humorous incident to life. Convinced that he is dying, Asbury insults his mother, a Methodist, by insisting she call to his bedside a minister of a high church background. The young man hopes to hold an intellectual, sophisticated discussion on theological matters that will essentially negate the Christian faith.

"It's so nice to have you come," Asbury says when the minister in collar enters the room. "This place is so intellectually dreary. There's no one here an intelligent person can talk to. I wonder, Sir, what you think of Joyce?"

"You'll have to shout a little louder," says the minister. "I'm blind in one eye and deaf in one ear. Joyce who?"

"James Joyce," responds the pretentious young writer.

"Never heard of him," says the minister. "Now. Do you say your morning and evening prayers?"

This delightfully whacky exchange continues for several pages.

"Don't pray, eh?" says the minister. "Well, you will never learn to be good unless you pray regularly."

"The myth of the dying god has always fascinated me," shouts the sick young man. But the minister did not catch it because he responds by saying again, "You must pray."

Asbury has an answer for this, "The artist prays by creating. . ."

"Not enough," snaps the minister.

Asbury slumps in the bed. "But I'm dying!" he shouts.

"You're not dead yet," says the minister. "And how do you expect to meet God face-to-face when you've never spoken to him! God does not send the Holy Ghost to those who don't ask for him. Ask him to send the Holy Ghost."

"The Holy Ghost!" responds Asbury. "That's the last thing I'm looking for."

The minister answers, "And he may be the last thing you get. . ."

As it happens, the minister is correct. The title "The Enduring Chill" is a reference to the Holy Ghost. The story ends this way: "Asbury blanched. . .he saw that for the rest of his days, frail and racked, he would live in the face of a purifying terror. A feeble cry, a last impossible protest escaped him. But the Holy Ghost emblazoned in ice, instead of fire, continued, implacable, to descend."

Asbury is like many people who ask, "How do I overcome my spiritual problems? How do I master the mature things of the Christian faith?" They don't particularly want a sincere answer; they want some sort of intellectual hocus-pocus, some kind of theorizing that sounds mystical and otherworldly.

So the answer most offensive to these people is: "Read your Bible and pray, and ask for the Holy Spirit to teach you."

In effect they reply, "I'm in the grips of a spiritual illness that may be terminal."

But the answer is basically the same: They must read their

Bible and pray and ask for the Holy Spirit to teach them. In their heart of hearts, they already know what to do. The same is true with people who have trouble with their tongues: they need to do what they already know to do. Read the Scripture, be obedient to what it says, pray continually about their tongue difficulties and ask the Holy Spirit to teach them to speak in a whole new Christ-like way.

Sometimes, however, they need a little help; they need to be shocked out of their spiritual apathy. They need an old one-eyed, one-eared minister to shout at them while they wallow in their figurative spiritual death beds.

One of the most effective tools I've discovered for helping me do what I already know to do is an accountability relationship. Webster defines *accountable* as "liable to be called to account or answerable to a superior."

In an accountability relationship, I define what I should be doing and am not doing and then invite someone to hold me accountable for growth in those areas. When David and I were still in the pastorate, I started a number of "growth groups" among the women in our church for the purpose of accelerating spiritual growth. These groups met for two months and had no more than six members.

Each person named the areas in which she needed to grow and then asked the group for help. For instance, a woman might say, "I just can't get into Scripture. There's so much else going on in my life. I need help." Then another woman might volunteer to call the first in the middle of the week to ask, "Have you found time to study your Bible yet?"

Accountability works like a charm. If I know someone is going to phone me at a certain time, it gives me tremendous impetus to do what I know I need to do.

The groups were dynamic spiritual accelerators. I saw women write out growth contracts with each other and share baby-sitting so they each would have time for Bible study, for prayer, and for seeking the things of the Spirit. In fact, the women's groups were so successful that the men began forming growth groups, holding each other accountable for spiritual growth.

But accountability doesn't have to involve a group. It can be a one-to-one relationship in which the two parties agree to encourage and hold each other to spiritual growth. Or it can be the kind of relationship where a person seeking spiritual growth asks a spiritual advisor to hold him or her accountable for growth in defined areas.

This process encompasses what Scripture means in its "one another" passages—love one another, care for one another, bear one another's burdens, and so on. Holding one another accountable is one of the ways that we fulfill Christ's law of love. And we can't fulfill it unless we know one another, know each other's pains and difficulties. Healing comes when someone tells us what we must do and then offers to walk along the way with us until the effort becomes a discipline. And eventually, the discipline does take over.

If we have determined that the diagnosis is correct, that we have mouth disease, then whom can we trust to hold us accountable? We need individually to say to this person, "I have trouble with my tongue." Then we need to define the symptoms. "I lose my temper. I gossip. I speak negatively. I talk too much." Then we must decide what needs to be done. Do we require minor surgery? Major surgery? Or do we simply need to work at tongue therapy, applying the rehabilitation exercises mentioned in the last chapters?

Doing what we already know we should do is a basic growth principle in Christian living, and speaking words of life to God or about God is a sign of verbal health.

My son, keep well thy tongue and keep thy friend.
A wicked tongue is worse than a fiend. . .
The first virtue, son, if thou wilt learn,
Is to restrain and keep well thy tongue.

Chaucer
"The Maunciple's Tale"

13

SPEAKING WORDS OF LIFE
TO OTHERS

We've undergone examination, diagnosed mouth disease, courageously submitted to surgery, both minor and major, and we've spent arduous time in rehabilitation. We've noticed definite improvement, a decrease in symptoms, a lessening of the wakeful night syndrome and holy words beginning to replace what was once unholy.

Now what?

What about the woman down the block? She just delivered her eleventh baby, looks fit as a fiddle at forty, is the first woman to dress her children in summer clothes when the season changes, never, I said *never* (all the houses are close enough to hear), raises her voice in anger, plays an instrument in the community symphony, teaches the deaf a couple of days a week, and shares regularly with her husband during a private hour over coffee after dinner (while the kid crew cleans up).

Did I ever really know such a paragon of virtue?

You betcha!

Maureen Reilley lived down the street from me when I had three children and was expecting my fourth, when my laundry room was always piled with overripe dirty clothes, when I never got into summer clothes until July, when the only time I spent with my pastor-husband was at church business meetings or sometimes while he was shaving.

You get the idea, I'm sure. Every woman knows at least one Maureen Reilley.

What's more, these superwomen rarely attend church, often dismiss God with a casual sophistication, or follow a brand of religion that isn't the evangelical, Bible-memorizing, church-every-Sunday kind of Christianity I grew up with and thought was the only valid kind in the world.

How do we, normal ordinary Christian men and women, just healing from violent cases of tongue dislocation, witness to the Maureen Reilleys (or to her male equivalents) of the world?

Well, first of all, let me make one thing perfectly clear; we cannot compete with the Maureen Reilleys of this world. Second, we will do much better touching the life of these superhumans on our block if we also scratch the word witness. Let me explain what I mean.

I am from the sweaty-palm, hit-them-with-a-tract-and-run school of evangelism. One experience from high school is prototypic of my whole relationship with the word witness. One non-Christian young man established a chat-after-school, can-I-give-you-a-lift home kind of friendship. He was a nice-looking young man, but I would never have thought of dating him because who knows what that would have led to—unequal yokeage, certainly.

He kept saying things like, "I've got these two tickets to the Spring Talent Night and wonder if you know a girl who would make a good date for the evening." I was so obtuse that I recommended a girl friend whose parents didn't mind her dating non-Christian fellows.

I kept telling this young man about Jesus Christ, making sure I had all the leading questions and procedures of witnessing correct (like an encyclopedia salesman). I also had tantalizing conversational materials to share with my friends (all Christian) about the guy in the popular group whom I was trying to win to Christ.

Never mind that I didn't have sense enough to know that he wanted to take *me* to the talent show and that I could have paid him an enormous compliment by saying, "I'm a girl who'd make a good date for the evening. Why don't you ask me?" Never mind that the dating prohibitions of my Christian subculture implied that if non-Christian fellows weren't sex fiends, they were certainly inferior company, and that I was better than they.

Never mind that two years after we graduated from high school, his parents died in the fire that burned their home, and I never found the time to write that note of comfort, which some urgent voice within kept impressing me to write.

Needless to say, my friend never became a Christian and in fact at our ten-year class reunion, he announced in a rather beery voice, "Well, Karen Burton! Here's the only girl who ever tried to win me to Christ!"

He did exactly what he intended to do. He mortified me.

He said the same thing ten years later at our twenty-year reunion, but this time he had gained thirty pounds and his eyes were filled with pain and frustration. His voice was more than beery; it was downright inebriated. This time he didn't mortify me—he dismissed me.

Through such casualties we learn painfully about witnessing.

My friend had a long memory. He knew in high school and remembered at our reunion that I didn't care a hoot about him as a person. I was just rattling off rote formulas that had nothing to do with him but everything to do with how my subculture measured the successfulness of my spiritual journey.

God forgive me.

So I have scratched the word witness—not that it isn't a good word. It's a wonderful word, but unfortunately it brings a knot to the pit of my stomach, sweaty palms, and an old voice from the past that whispers, "You've got to be as good, if not better, than the world for people to respect you as a Christian." Phooey!

I have since been learning how to use this mouth to speak Christ's life to this world.

When one's daughter goes through high school, one begins to experience *déjà vu*. At the beginning of her senior year, my daughter transferred from the local private Christian school to the public high school. This was not a protest movement; I suspect Melissa just needed to try her wings in a less sheltered, more challenging environment.

She often came home with poignant stories about some of the girls who had taken a break in their schooling to have a baby and had returned, and were jamming their senior studies between midnight feedings and new, too early marriages.

I can remember girls like that from my past, only they didn't come back to school. They were the kind of girls one had to be careful about associating with because "one might tarnish one's own reputation."

Melissa didn't seem to be too concerned about her own reputation. She seemed to be more concerned about the feelings and struggles of her young friends. "Mother, Wendy's parents won't even let her bring her baby home. They aren't talking to her. She's living with her new in-laws, but I don't think it's working out very well."

No one had told Melissa that her reason for being at the public high school was "to win the school for Christ." In fact, that was *not* the basic reason she was where she was. Her purpose was to learn who Melissa was, what her world was like, and then to integrate the one into the other. She had not mapped out an evangelistic program for her high school friends. She did not, like her mother before her, carry a big red Bible on top of her books.

But she was a far better witness than I ever was, although I don't think I heard her use the word.

She used a lot of synonyms for the word witness. She said the word listen as in "I listened" or "I just listened." She said, "I care about. . ." She asked, "How can I help? What can I do for . . . ?" She used the word friend over and over: "Mother, I made a new friend today," or "I keep having all these different kinds of people say to me, 'I've never had a best friend like you.'"

I wonder if Melissa's approach would work with the Maureen Reilleys down the block?

How about an experiment? First, scratch the word witness. Then, think a brand new thought: Maybe you weren't placed on your block to win Maureen Reilley (or in the office to win her husband, Ted) to the Lord, but maybe Maureen Reilley was placed on your block to teach you how to be a better mother, wife, and person.

Admit it: that woman can teach you a thing or two. Swallow your pride. Bake some banana bread. Knock on her door and say, "Hey, lady. Either today, tomorrow, or the next day, I need to spend some time with you. How in the world do you do all you do?"

Maureen Reilley will love it. Any woman would!

Then listen to everything she has to tell you. Ask questions and listen some more. Put away your competitiveness and learn to care for her as a person. As she talks and tells you about herself, you may discover areas in which you can help her. (Offer to take care of that eleventh baby. The woman may be a paragon of virtue, but after all, she doesn't have twelve arms.)

Since the witnessing debacles of my younger years, I've discovered a whole new twist to my tongue on this topic. I'm a much better witness when I'm listening than when I'm telling. In other words, my relationship with people begins with my wanting to know them. This means asking questions such as: Who are you? What do you do for a living? What do you do with your leisure time? Do you have any intellectual interests? What are your children doing?

For me, witnessing begins with listening, laughing, sympathizing deeply, and waiting for the Holy Spirit to direct. Invariably, when I do listen, the conversation turns to significant spiritual topics.

This last month, I talked to two strangers. One was an older woman who revealed she was afraid of death. I told her I had once been afraid of the same thing, but then I realized that if I was truly a Christian, Christ would take away that fear and he had. She sighed deeply, patted my hand, and said, "I know God put you beside me to comfort me." No sweaty palms there.

The other person was a college student who revealed she was sickened by the empty traditions of her childhood faith and suspected that the religious life of her parents was mostly habit. I told her I knew exactly what she meant and that the struggle from religious forms into a truly religious life had been the thrust of my spiritual journey. But I also told her that I had discovered that Christ, the everburning flame in the soul of each person who believes, can become the center of faith.

"That's beautiful," she replied. "I needed to hear you say that. It gives me hope."

So you see, my tales of witnessing aren't all failures. I have learned some things in these forty years of life and twenty-some years since high school. I have learned that witnessing begins with caring and with the questions: Who is this person? What does he or she hope to be?

Along the way, I have made other amazing discoveries. I have found that although the world is full of remarkable people, there are really no Maureen Reilleys. There is no one in our broken world who is untouched by that world. We are all imperfect people.

Everyone has a hidden handicap that he or she needs to hear another accept by saying, "That doesn't matter to me. What matters to me is what and who you are right now." Everyone has experienced death—the death of a relationship, a dream, or a loved one. Many, many, many have undergone traumatic emotional or physical violation.

I have scratched the word witnessing from my functional vocabulary and that has helped me to discard the rigid impositions and misconceptions that crushed the life of that word. This linguistic modification freed me tremendously. I have also scratched the unrealistic idea that I have to be a perfect Christian woman. I am not, cannot be, and never will be perfect, this side of heaven. This realization, too, has liberated me from cloying human pride.

It is from my humanity that I speak the words of Christ-life. I know why that woman down the block is driven to perfection; it is because she is afraid to be found imperfect. That fear was once mine. We are united in our humanity. And I know that Christ loves me even as I wallow in my humanness.

So it doesn't matter if I can't make a batch of cookies without doubling something I shouldn't and invariably eliminating an essential ingredient. It doesn't matter that I fight phone phobia and seem harsh at moments when I'm preoccupied. I am not witnessing to myself. I am witnessing to the One who is all that matters.

All of the world may be able to get through this moment and the next without Christ, but I, imperfect and often misfunctioning, cannot. I need him from this breath to the next. Out of my incompleteness I witness to completeness. Out of our common humanity, I speak of the uncommon humanity of Another.

I am glad my daughter is not afraid to be her whacky,

irrepressible self. I was so inhibited as a high schooler that I had a ghetto mentality. Everyone was my enemy, my potential oppressor. I had to prove myself to them.

"Why are you always so much fun?" my daughter's friends ask her. "What are you high on today?"

One of Melissa's breezy replies is, "Oh, today I'm high on jelly beans!" Another is "I'm high on Jesus and I'm gonna live forever!"

"What do your friends say to *that?*" I want to know—really want to know.

"Oh, first they laugh because they think I'm joking, then they sort of go 'Whaa-a-a-a-a-a—did that girl say what I think she said, and do I think she really means it?'"

It's a marvelous answer from this tongue freed from ecclesiastical prohibitions, an answer out of Melissa's irrepressible humanity. But I know exactly what she means. Some days I'm a little whacky with the jelly bean side of life, but most of the time, I'm high on Jesus. Eternal life began for me when the warm flame within began to flicker higher.

And I know that more and more this tongue is going to be able to speak the words of life; I care, I love, I hear.

I'm sure the woman down the block knows all there is to know about life's jelly bean side as well. One day, perhaps, as I listen, respond, and befriend her, she'll want to know about the warm flame within, and maybe, popping jelly beans together, I'll tell her.

Wel you know every now and agen youwl hear some thing it means what ever it means but youwl know theres mor in it as wel. Moren were knowit by who ever said it. So that reveal stayd in my mynd. . .You see how it wer up to then I never thot this Legend ben anything moren a picter story about a bloak with a name near the same as Eusa. Nor I din't know nothing of chemistery nor fizzics then I hadnt payd no tension to it. Any how I were reading over this here Legend like I use to do some times and I come to "the figure of the crucified Saviour." Number of the crucified Saviour and wunnering how that be come the Little Shyning Man the Addom.

Russell Hoban
Riddley Walker

14

SPEAKING WORDS OF LIFE TO OUR CULTURE

In the play *Children of a Lesser God,* James Leeds, a speech pathologist, comes to teach in a state school for the deaf, where he meets, falls in love with and eventually marries a student, Sarah Norman, who has been deaf from birth.

"What is it like in your silence?" he asks. She signs her answer: "Deafness isn't the opposite of hearing as you think. It's a silence full of sound. The sound of spring breaking up through the deafness of winter."

Children of a Lesser God is a poignant play about deafness and speech, but it's also about much more. It is about the translation, the interpretation of language that occurs in every human relationship.

In the play Sarah makes an impassioned speech using sign langauge, which is translated on stage by the actor who plays her husband.

> For all my life I have been the creation of other people.
> The first thing I was ever able to understand was that

everyone was supposed to hear but I couldn't and that was bad. Then they told me everyone was supposed to be smart but I was dumb. Then they said, Oh no, I wasn't permanently dumb, only temporarily, but to be smart I had to become an imitation of the people who had from birth everything a person has to have to be good: ears that hear, mouth that speaks, eyes that read, brain that understands.

Well, my brain understands a lot; and my eyes are my ears; and my hands are my voice; and my language, my speech, my ability to communicate is as great as yours. Greater, maybe, because I can communicate to you in one image an idea more complex than you can speak in fifty words.

The dilemma of these two lovers and protagonists, James and Sarah, is that James wants Sarah to speak using words, his language, the language of the hearing and she refuses. The climax of the play comes when James forces his wife to try speech.

Shut up! You want to talk to me, then you learn my language! Did you get that? Of course you did. You've probably been reading lips perfectly for years; but it's a great control game, isn't it? You can cook, but you can't speak. You can drive and shop but you can't speak. You can even make a speech but you still can't do it alone. Now come on! I want you to speak to me. Let me hear it. Speak! Speak! Speak!

At this point in the play, Sarah erupts into anguished imitation of human language, the sound of which appalls the audience—then she rushes from the stage and leaves her husband.

In the last years I have found myself in the far-flung corners of the world. In 1980 while surveying the refugee camps in Pakistan, waiting for the end of a three-way translation, from Farsi, to Pakistani, to English, in the midst of a mob of excited Afghanistan refugees traumatized by their recent border escape,

I had one brief thought: It is we who are the interpreters of Christ to the world.

Each time since, waiting for the translation of the Thai, Vietnamese, or Hebrew languages, I have again been impressed with more impelling clarity—we as Christians must translate the Word to the world. Yet as Christians we have much the same difficulty in communicating the Word, Christ, as James Leeds did communicating his frustration to his wife, Sarah.

A friend, who is a speech pathologist, shared the steps it took to teach a deaf child the meaning of the word *dog.* The learning process begins with a picture of a dog. The deaf child must learn to sign, using his hands, the symbol for dog. Then he must learn to write it in block letters and in cursive; next he must learn to read lips. Even after this process, when that deaf child sees a real dog, he often is unable to recognize this wiggling, furry creature as being the same as the picture, the sign, the block and cursive letter, and the movement of lips. He will have to be taught that a big German shepherd is a dog, a toy poodle is a dog, and so on.

Now imagine: if these are the complications of teaching one simple word to the deaf that represents something that can be seen, touched, and smelled, how difficult must it be to convey the meaning of something abstract that cannot be seen, touched, or smelled—like the word *God.*

One of the reasons for such dismal effects in personal evangelism is that we keep shouting like James Leeds, "Speak! Speak! Speak!" Use my symbols. Struggle with my language. Be like me. But like Sarah, deaf from birth, this nonhearing society cannot understand the words of the church.

According to my friend, one out of twenty people have some kind of hearing loss. That means out of three hundred people, twenty will have some difficulty with sound.

There are two types of hearing losses, all in varying degrees from mild to severe. The first type of debility is one in which the sufferer just can't hear words loudly enough. Aided by a hearing device words are now louder, but so are all accessory noises—nearby traffic, background conversations, dishes, radio music. Diminished hearing is not quite as easy to correct with a mechanical aid as most of us think.

The other type of loss is when one can hear the words but not understand them. Making the words louder will not help; a hearing aid will not help. To someone with this intelligibility problem, the word welcome sounds like oca. Shouting or turning up the hearing device makes that word seem like OCA. One solution to this hearing difficulty is utilizing sign language. Sign language is the fourth largest foreign language in America.

The prophets of old all cried: "You have eyes to see but do not see. You have ears to hear but do not hear!" That describes our world as well. Communicating to a non-Christian culture is much the same as communicating with the deaf.

Every missionary knows that when he travels to a foreign land to take the message of Christ, he must first learn the language of that land. He must understand the culture, its habits, its meanings, and its idioms. The missionary must first be an anthropologist, studying the meaning of man in that environment. He must abandon his western mentality of falsely assumed superiority and first be a learner. It is the culture that teaches him. He has the message of life, but in order to communicate that message, he must become the student.

So must we Christians. In order to interpret Christ to our alien culture, we must understand its language and its symbols.

Carl R. Rogers writes:

> Can I let myself enter fully into the world of another's feelings and personal meanings and see these as he or she does? Can I step into his or her private world so completely that I lose all desire to evaluate or judge it? Can I enter it so sensitively that I can move about in it freely without trampling on meanings that are precious? Can I sense it so

accurately that I can catch not only the meanings of experience which are obvious to him or her, but these meanings which are only implicit, which he sees only dimly or as confusion?

Mouth disease is responding to treatment when we put down our obnoxious rush to tell, and through deep, concerned prayer discover the best way to translate the Word, Christ, to the world. We do this through verbal witness, through mouths that are incarnated with Christ's mouth, and through the witness of righteous and loving lives. We must also struggle to understand what our culture is saying so we can use the very symbols they hold dear, sign to them, if you please, the meaning of Christ in the language they understand.

In the book *Peace Child*, Don Richardson tells about his missionary experience with the Sawi tribe in New Guinea, headhunting cannibals who pillowed their heads on the skulls of their victims. Among these people, treachery was more than a way of life; it was a heroic ideal. To fatten a victim with friendship for the purpose of slaughter was regarded as the highest type of treachery, a form to be venerated. The heroes of the Sawi legends were not those warriors mighty in battle, but those who achieved the most sublime betrayal—that which led to eventual murder. How were the Richardsons to convey the gospel message of Christ's redemptive love to a people who would consider Judas the hero for betraying his friend with a kiss?

In time, another custom was discovered that opened the way for the gospel message. Among the Sawi, every demonstration of friendship was suspect except one. As a sign of peace between warring tribes, two infants would be traded and as long as these two lived, the warring parties would honor their armistice. If a man would actually give his son to his enemies, that man could be trusted. The Richardsons told the story of how God gave his Peace Child to a hostile earth revolting against him in enemy rebellion, and this striking cultural analogy opened the way for the good news of the gospel in that tribe.

In his book, Richardson includes a moving prayer:

> I thank You, my Father, for laying the groundwork for our ministry to these people. The Sawi were strangers to our Judeo-Christian heritage, yet You so providentially ordained these redemptive analogies within their culture ages ago so that one day we would find and use them for Your glory. You were concerned, not only to send messengers, but also to prepare a culture to receive their message. . .As You prepared the Hebrews and the Greeks, so also the Sawi were not too insignificant or too pagan to receive this much of Your providence.

Don Richardson goes on to maintain that every culture has its redemptive analogies, customs, traditions, even myths that God has planted within the culture that can be pointers to him. He elaborates on this even further in his next book *Eternity in Their Hearts.*

Like the missionary, we must understand that we live in an alien culture. If we are going to translate the Word to our world while speaking uncommon spiritual truths in a common language, we are going to have to struggle with its symbols and signs.

The words spoken to a neighbor, "We'd love to have you come to church with us," may evoke irrational responses. They may conjure up old stereotypes and unfortunate unpleasantries. If we want our neighbors to respond to Christ, we are going to have to walk in their worlds for awhile until we can determine the right redemptive analogy.

When we enter into this communication struggle, we become Christ-like. Christ took on our symbol, human flesh, so that we could understand God's language. He became like us, human. He entered into our culture. He became the redemptive analogy of all time. This divine action of taking on flesh was the archetypical action of all time. He became proficient in our signs so that we could eventually know the language of the soul.

For me, as a writer, this concept has forced me into years of intensive study and reading in order to prepare myself to write for that spiritually nonhearing reader. I have spent over ten years searching through secular literature to determine which are the best ways to speak this Word and to ascertain which are the redemptive analogies in our twentieth-century time.

While attending a lecture by the psychiatrist and best-selling author, F. Scott Peck, I became aware of the redemptive potential of sex in our culture. He recalled the myth from Plato's *Symposium* about men having been originally hermaphroditic until the gods split them in half and how as half-creatures they were no longer able to compete with the gods. Peck then went on to explain that this sense of incompleteness, this longing for the other self, this search for wholeness, which results in multiplied sexual encounters, is the closest many people ever come to a religious experience. Whether they are aware of it or not, this hunger and searching is a hunger for God. Why else, he asked, should sexuality be complicated with reverence?

In Scripture sexual love is a robust symbol for a yet more robust love. Robert Capon has said, "Since God created man in his own image and since man is a sexual being, God is also sexual." My notes from Peck's lecture read:

> God is the Divine Seducer who is always seducing us. In a sense He is a God who is always on the make. We have been brought to bed, caught, deflowered spiritually. . .he loves us beyond belief, wants us, will have us. . .spirituality and sexuality lie so close to each other, it's impossible to invoke one without invoking the other.

Christ understood that the Samaritan woman with five husbands was searching for meaning in her very sin. She was thirsty, parched, a dry gourd emptied to receive overdue rain. He used her symbol of inner drought and pointed her to the only one who could quench her thirstiness, himself, the Living Water.

So can we. Though sex in our culture has become perverted and we have filled our media and our minds with depravity, sex, at its deepest level, is a search for intimacy, holiness, and union, which can only, ultimately, be found in God. People are crying, "We want something more, something infinitely deeper, something so soulish, so satisfying, it is beyond our imaginings!"

It is we, like the Richardsons, who are speaking to a tribal culture, though technologically advanced; it is we who must make the dementia sane, the sacrilege holy once again, finding the words to speak in a way the world understands, "Are you hungry, athirst, desperate for union? Are your human joinings empty, meaningless? You can find fulfillment in Christ. He will give you an intimacy of the soul that can be given by no other."

It is the Christian who translates the Word, Christ, to this spiritually deaf world. And in order to do so, some of us are going to have to expose ourselves to what the culture of the world around us is saying. We must discriminately and carefully educate ourselves in language study and we must do it in a way in which we ourselves do not lose our spiritual perceptions.

This is a very tall order.

Several rules have helped me these last years as I have listened to the language of my own culture in order to be able to translate Christ using its own symbols. First, I choose samples of this culture to study that are the best forms of expression of my culture. I read the best authors and see the best art. I do not wallow in muck for wallowing in muck's sake; it soon sickens me.

Then I discipline myself to spend a proportionate amount of time in studying the language of heaven through prayer, Bible study, and reading spiritual classics. A journey into my culture without a commensurate journey into the spiritual life would be damaging to me. I might lose my usefulness as a translator.

Then I pray for understanding. What is the meaning of the things I have seen and heard and how can they be used redemptively? Many Christians were upset with the motion picture *ET* because of what they felt were occultish derivatives. For the sake of all the children of my acquaintance who saw the film and who never attend church, I would prefer to focus on the fact that there was a strong Christ-figure in the extraterrestial who came to earth, taught earthlings to love in a new way, died, came back to life, and left promising his presence.

Now it is my turn to turn the tale true, holy, and to focus eyes wide with fantasy to the Extraterrestrial who came and is coming again. (An interviewer asked Stephen Spielberg, the producer of this film, if *ET* wasn't a Christ figure. The scriptwriter, a Catholic woman, responded affirmatively to which Spielberg exclaimed, "Oh, no, don't say that! I'm Jewish!")

God will make his message known. Truth will win out. It may have gathered the accumulated barnacles of error and hostility; it may be a shining gemstone in a manure pile; but we can find it, we can use it, we can turn the hearts of men, women, and children to it.

I find useable redemptive analogies in our secularized, human-centered culture all the time. Last fall, I had gone to bed with a nasty grippe. David was traveling; the children all had weekend plans; and after the initial physical distress, I felt restless, but too weak to try a major project.

The movie *Mad Max: Beyond Thunderdome* was playing (cheaply) nearby, and the reviews had been surprisingly good. Since my mental and physical lassitude needed non-demanding activity, I took myself off to a local theater (the one I wasn't allowed to enter during my childhood and adolescence because of a religious stricture).

Mad Max is the third in a trilogy of films all set in time after a nuclear holocaust. Max is a survivor who finds himself in the incredible dregs-of-life flea market of Bartertown ruled by Aunty Entity, another survivor. He is hired to liquidate a rival for her power but must do so according to an emerging primitive code in the battle arena, the Thunderdome, where the rule is: "Two men enter, one man leaves!" The fight commences; but Max discovers he has been duped and refuses to kill his opponent, so he is banished to the Desert of Despair.

Near death, as the sands cover his prostrate figure, he is rescued by desert children, a remnant band of survivors who have reverted to near primitive conditions and are living by a stream in greening Eden-like innocence. They have an oral tradition, a "Tell," which sustains their belief in future deliverance and keeps alive remnant memory of their past.

At this part of the movie, my heart leapt, old analogy hunter that I have become. The children reiterate the Tell in a survivor's lingo. Savannah, the heroine, takes the Tell, "I's lookin' behind us now across the count of time. Down the long haul. . .into history and back. I sees the end what were the start. It's the Pox-Eclipse, full of pain. . . ." Her story proceeds until she comes to the part where Max is involved. A group of civilians had escaped the nuclear blast by flight and landed in this green spa in the desert. Eventually some of them attempted to return. She points to the words etched on a stone wall: RESCUE PARTY, DEPARTED ON THE 8.11.05. LED BY FLIGHT CAPTAIN G. L. WALKER. Savannah continued the Tell, "They said bidy-bye to them what they birthed. And from out of the nothing they looked back, and Captain Walker hollered: 'Wait. One of us will come.'"

Of course, the children believe that Max is the promised deliverer Captain Walker, and this belief catapults him and them into a fantastic adventure of challenge, chase, and rescue with Max symbolically laying down his life for their escape.

The film ends in a blasted towering city, a crumbling remembrance of what has been, with Savannah drawing other survivors near at day's end in a vast hall lit by dim fires burning in braziers and proclaiming:

> One look and we knowed we got it straight—those what had gone before had the knowin' and the doin' of things beyond our reckonin'. . .even beyond our dreamin'. . .Time counts and keeps countin' and we knows now—findin' the trick of what's been and lost ain't no easy ride. But that's our track, we gotta travel it, and there ain't nobody knows where it's gonna lead.
>
> Still and all, every night we does the Tell, so that we'll all 'member who we was and where we came from. . .But most of all we 'members the man who finded us, him that came the salvage. . .And we lights the beacons, but not just for him—for all of 'em that are still out there. . .'Cos we knows there'll come a night when they sees the flickering light, and they'll be coming home. . . .

By this time, every creative nerve-ending within me was alive, my eyes filled with tears in that darkened theater because I know I am a teller of the Tell. I and others like me are the ones who keep alive the memory of him who became salvage for us, and we fire the wordlights bright, build up the bonfire with kindling of words, phrases, and paragraphs, flap glowing charcoals with our hand bellows, and we cradle dying embers with warm breathing thoughts for him, for him, but also (in Savannah's words) "for them what is birthed and them what is unbirthed" so these flickering lights will be seen. And because of us, some night, some night soon or some night down the track of history, they'll be coming home.

When I think of words and their potential power, when I think of speaking Christ into the ears of hearers, and when I think of writing for long, lonely hours, I am often tempted by the thought: What difference will it make? My words are so few in contrast to the many that speak lies, unholiness, despair, and hatred. How can I impress on my children the power, the life-giving value of godly words? How can I make them understand the sacramental actuality of words greatly conceived and expressed? How shall I respond if they too ask: What difference will it make?

Thorton Wilder, the playwright of *Our Town* and *The Skin of Our Teeth*, and a man who grappled with his own inadequate humanity and was creatively blocked for much of his life, responds to the question "What difference can I make?" as well as any in his book *The Angel That Troubled the Waters, and Other Plays*. To it I lend my own grateful affirmation.

> You say the little efforts that I make
> Will do no good; they never will prevail
> To tip the hovering scale
> Where justice hangs in balance.
> I don't think
> I ever thought they would.
>
> But I am prejudiced beyond debate
> In favor of my right to choose which side
> Shall feel the stubborn ounces of my weight.

There is power in the tongue, power of life or death.

Oh, God, give our tongues the words that will translate the Word to this world.

Seventy years are given to us! And some may even live to eighty. But even the best of these years are often emptiness and pain; soon they disappear, and we are gone. Teach us to number our days and recognize how few they are; help us to spend them as we should.

—Psalm 90:10, 12 LB

APPENDIX
Curative Aids

THE TONGUE DIAGNOSTIC EXAMINATION

Give yourself a tongue checkup in the following five areas. Check the statements in each of the self-diagnostic sections that describe your tongue condition.

SILENCE

"A time to keep silence, and a time to speak" (Eccl. 3:7).

☐ In an empty house, I turn on the TV even when I'm not in the room just to fill the silence.

☐ I frequently return home after social evenings thinking I've talked too much.

☐ If there is a gap in conversation, I tend to fill it with words.

☐ During times of silence in church, my mind thinks of all the things I need to do.

☐ I use the phone as a security blanket.

☐ The thought of a three-day retreat in silence overwhelms me.

☐ During interpersonal crises, I often don't know how to find words of wisdom to speak.

☐ I rarely hear the inner voice of the Lord speaking to me. I don't understand this.

☐ I often wish I had said things I didn't say, or I wish I hadn't said what I did say.

☐ I do not know how to use silence well to enhance my habits of speaking.

☐ I often feel guilty about repeating things I suspect I shouldn't repeat.

☐ In conversations, I think more about how I'm going to respond than listening.

WORDS OF AFFIRMATION

"Let no evil talk come out of your mouths, but only such as is good for edifying, as fits the occasion, that it may impart grace to those who hear" (Eph. 4:29).

☐ I feel things deeply within, but I choke when I attempt to speak about them.

☐ My own parents rarely said they loved me or that I had done well.

☐ I'm afraid if I affirm my children, they'll become proud.

☐ I affirm, but then I can't resist the temptation to add a little dig.

☐ I'm afraid if I affirm the people close to me, they'll take advantage of me.

☐ Actions speak louder than words; my family knows that I love them without my words.

☐ I never hear God's words of affirmation. I do hear him say, "Do more."

☐ I think about writing thank-you notes; then most of the time I forget.

☐ Our dinner table times are frequently family gripe sessions.

☐ Few people ever say good things to me; why should I do this for others?

WORDS AS GIFTS

"To one is given through the Spirit the utterance of wisdom. . .to another the utterance of knowledge"(1 Cor. 12:8).

☐ I frequently find myself being as catty with church people as with anyone else.

☐ I rarely talk about spiritual things with church people.

☐ Some people in the church I'm angry with; some I don't want to speak to.

☐ Let's face it; I gossip about people in the church. (I don't call it gossip, but it is.)

☐ I know how to deal a blow; I don't use my fists, but my humor can be deadly.

☐ I often feel as though not many people in the church care about me.

☐ I don't understand how words can be used to bring supernatural comfort.

☐ The minister should take care of speaking spiritual words; laypeople should listen.

☐ Some of the deepest wounds to me have come from the words of church people.

☐ Wouldn't it be thrilling if I knew that Christ was speaking through my mouth?

☐ I have a friend who always says the right word; I would love to be like that.

KEEPING YOUR WORD

"Let your yes be yes and your no be no, that you may not fall under condemnation" (James 5:12).

☐ Often I say I'll do things but then I forget or I don't feel like it anymore.

☐ I just plain can't decide; often I want to and I don't want to—at the same time.

☐ When I'm saying the actual words, I know that's not what I want to say.

☐ I have a habit of saying what I know people want to hear just to please them.

☐ I tend to exaggerate the truth either by loading it with emotion or by stretching facts.

☐ I can't think of a person to describe as one who keeps his word.

☐ I frequently say a casual statement like "let's get together" without meaning it.

☐ I make personal resolves but have difficulty following through on them.

☐ I have a need to always explain myself, endlessly justifying what I say and do.

☐ I rarely take other people at face value; there's got to be more behind their words.

ADMITTING YOUR FAULTS

"If we confess our sins, he is faithful and just, and will forgive our sins and cleanse us from all unrighteousness" (1 John 1:9).

☐ I feel like I have to defend myself from attack, even with positive criticism.

☐ I rarely apologize to my friends. I hope they'll overlook my faults.

☐ I'm afraid that if I admit my errors people will, in some way, abandon me.

☐ I feel that everything about me is wrong, though I wouldn't admit this to friends.

☐ I haven't often felt the release of saying "I'm sorry" to man or God.

☐ Prayers of confession are words that I too often say by rote.

☐ I often feel guilt and I'm not sure why.

☐ When I pray, my words seem like lead ballons.

☐ I can't remember when I heard God personally whisper to my ear, "You're forgiven."

☐ It would be wonderful to be finally free of this inward burden of having to justify myself.

THE PRAYER

Lord,
Examine me.
Teach me what it is I say
That speaks death in my world.
Teach me what is unsaid
That can speak life.
Give unto me
Epiphanies of truth
At this moment of
Self-examination
I pray.
Amen.

THE TIME TEST: A LIE TREATMENT

If we diagnose our tongue trouble as a tendency to tell untruths, good lie treatment occurs when we take an honest look at how we really use our time. Many of the lies we tell (i.e. I don't have enough time; I have too much to do) are shown to be bald-faced prevarications in the light of honest time-usage evaluations. An honest look at our daily habits, our work systems, our life management as it relates to time is a good place to begin to determine if the words we are saying are absolutely true.

A. *Take the Time Test.* You must commit yourself to 14 days.
B. *Gather your equipment.* Bring absolute honesty to the Time Test. If you cheat, you will only steal self-knowledge from yourself. Then choose a two week time-logging period. Start tomorrow, if possible, or on the weekend. Buy a notebook or allot a piece of paper for each day. Put the date at the top of each page.

ASSIGNMENT 1

C. *Time Test Pre-evaluation:* Fill in the following blanks.
   1. I wish I had more time for _____, but I don't.
   2. I spend very little time _____ _____.
   3. The major portion of my free time is spent _____ _____.
   4. I have _____ time to develop a spiritual life.
   5. I use the time that I have _____.

ASSIGNMENT 2

D. *Two-Week Log Time:* Now keep a log of your time. You can choose to log by the activity or by the hour. Activity logging might look like this:

Monday, Nov. 12

Getting dressed	1 hour	Studying	2 hours
Morning hassle	1 hour	Lunch	½ hour
Housework	1 hour	Shopping	2 hours

Hour logging might look like this:

Tuesday, Nov. 13

Work	12:30–4:30	Watching TV	8:00–9:00
Commuting	4:30–5:30	Housework	9:00–11:00
Dinner and clean up	6:00–8:00	Devotions	11:00–11:30

Extra Instructions for Time Logging:

1. Do not allow yourself to subconsciously alter your activities because you know you're going to have to record them. Behave in your normal manner.
2. Discipline yourself to record every minute. The tendency will be to underlog rather than to overlog.

ASSIGNMENT 3

E. *Assessing the Realities*

Go through your time log and total the results. How much cumulative time did you spend reading? Day-dreaming? Watching television? Baking? Working? Doing other things? Combine the various results in various categories. Some of your categories may overlap. "Time on the phone" and "Lunch with Ann" could be lumped together as "Time spent with friends."

Be sure to study your results carefully. Are there any patterns of which you were unaware? Were you surprised by any of the totals? Think about what this test reveals about YOU.

ASSIGNMENT 4

F. Breaking the Fictions

Now look over the totals you assessed for Assignment 3. Arrange these categories in the following space, putting the activity with the most total time (MTT) at the top of the list, and the activity with the least total time (LTT) at the bottom of the list.

MTT 1.

     2.

     3.

     4.

     5.

     6.

     7.

     8.

     9.

LTT 10.

Now answer the following questions:

1. Why do I devote so much time to the activities at the top of the list? Look carefully at how you spend your free time.

2. Compare your MTT's with the pre-evaluation statements you made at the beginning of the Time Test. Ask yourself: Does the real way I use my time verify these statements or contradict them?

3. Now make a painful evaluation: Am I using my time well? Are there time-consuming activities that have little or no worth and could be eliminated? Are there chunks of free time that are not being used in any profitable way at all? Am I spending too much time in a worthwhile pursuit that is nevertheless keeping me from activities that would be more profitable to me?

4. Write some evaluation statements in the following space. For instance: I spend too much time _____. I need to change _____

_____
_____.

I am going to _____.

5. Pray the following prayer:

God,
Help me to come to terms with time—what I do with it and how I use it. Help me to see that there is time enough for anything I really want to do. Help me to understand where I am telling lies, the lies of intent, the lies of self-negligence. May this test be a tool to measure if what I say is absolutely true.

Amen.

DAILY DOSES FROM PROVERBS

If you have become convinced that words have power and have now undergone a tongue examination to discover the severity of your own mouth disease, these thirty-one daily readings from the book of Proverbs will serve as a powerful medicament. A morning prayer is also included to read along with the daily doses. On page 219 there is an evening prayer of confession that can also be used for the end of each day.

Undergo this thirty-one day treatment cycle and if symptoms persist, repeat for another thirty-one day period.

DAY ONE

Chapter 4

O Lord, Guard my mouth today; say to me what to say.

20–22 My son, be attentive to my words;
    incline your ear to my sayings.
    Let them not escape from your sight;
    keep them within your heart.
    For they are life to him who finds them,
    and healing to all his flesh.

24   Put away from you crooked speech,
    and put devious talk far from you.

DAY TWO

Chapter 5

O Lord, May my lips be your lips; may my thoughts be yours I pray.

2   that you may keep discretion,
    and your lips may guard knowledge.

3–4 For the lips of a loose woman drip honey,
and her speech is smoother than oil;
but in the end she is bitter as wormwood,
sharp as a two-edged sword.

7 And now, O sons, listen to me,
and do not depart from the words of my mouth.

13 I did not listen to the voice of my teachers
or incline my ear to my instructors.

DAY THREE
Chapter 6
O Lord, Heal my heart so my lips will speak life.

12–14 A worthless person, a wicked man,
goes about with crooked speech,
winks with his eyes, scrapes with his feet,
points with his finger,
with perverted heart devises evil.

16–19 There are six things which the LORD hates,
seven which are an abomination to him:
haughty eyes, a lying tongue,
and hands that shed innocent blood,
a heart that devises wicked plans,
feet that make haste to run to evil,
a false witness who breathes out lies,
and a man who sows discord among brothers.

DAY FOUR
Chapter 7
O Lord, Let love be on my tongue; let it tell the words you tell.

1–3   My son, keep my words
and treasure up my commandments with you;
keep my commandments and live,
keep my teachings as the apple of your eye;
bind them on your fingers,
write them on the tablet of your heart.

DAY FIVE

Chapter 8

O Lord, Help me to refrain from speaking when silence is better.

6–8   Hear, for I will speak noble things,
and from my lips will come what is right;
for my mouth will utter truth;
wickedness is an abomination to my lips.
All the words of my mouth are righteous;
there is nothing twisted or crooked in them.

13   The fear of the LORD is hatred of evil.
Pride and arrogance and the way of evil
and perverted speech I hate.

DAY SIX

Chapter 9

O Lord, Give me the grace to say I'm sorry; it is my fault alone.

13   A foolish woman is noisy;
she is wanton and knows no shame.

DAY SEVEN

Chapter 10

O Lord, May I speak your words today, in your way.

11   The mouth of the righteous is a fountain of life,
        but the mouth of the wicked conceals violence.

14   Wise men lay up knowledge,
        but the babbling of a fool brings ruin near.

18–21   He who conceals hatred has lying lips,
        and he who utters slander is a fool.
        When words are many, transgression is not lacking,
        but he who restrains his lips is prudent.
        The tongue of the righteous is choice silver;
        the mind of the wicked is of little worth.
        The lips of the righteous feed many,
        but fools die for lack of sense.

DAY EIGHT

Chapter 10

O Lord, Christ in my speaking; Christ in my saying; Christ in my silence; Christ in today.

31–32   The mouth of the righteous brings forth wisdom,
        but the perverse tongue will be cut off.
        The lips of the righteous know what is acceptable,
        but the mouth of the wicked, what is perverse.

DAY NINE

Chapter 11

O Lord, Help me to break silence if words will heal.

9   With his mouth the godless man would destroy his
        neighbor,
        but by knowledge the righteous are delivered.

11   By the blessing of the upright a city is exalted,
      but it is overthrown by the mouth of the wicked.

12–13 He who belittles his neighbor lacks sense,
      but a man of understanding remains silent.
      He who goes about as a talebearer reveals secrets,
      but he who is trustworthy in spirit keeps a thing hidden.

DAY TEN
Chapter 12

O Lord, Help me to listen to others today as though you were listening to me.

6   The words of the wicked lie in wait for blood,
      but the mouth of the upright delivers men.

13–14 An evil man is ensnared by the transgression of his lips,
      but the righteous escapes from trouble.
      From the fruit of his words a man is satisfied with good,
      and the work of a man's hand comes back to him.

DAY ELEVEN
Chapter 13

O Lord, Give me the courage today to say I love.

2–3   From the fruit of his mouth a good man eats good,
      but the desire of the treacherous is for violence.
      He who guards his mouth preserves his life;
      he who opens wide his lips comes to ruin.

DAY TWELVE
Chapter 14

O Lord, Heal my heart; heal my tongue; heal my speaking.

3   The talk of a fool is a rod for his back,
     but the lips of the wise will preserve them.

5   A faithful witness does not lie,
     but a false witness breathes out lies.

7   Leave the presence of a fool,
     for there you do not meet words of knowledge.

23   In all toil there is profit,
     but mere talk tends only to want.

DAY THIRTEEN

Chapter 15

O Lord, May I speak words of beauty, peace, and praise; help me to refuse to utter any that negate, cancel, or destruct.

1–2 A soft answer turns away wrath,
     but a harsh word stirs up anger.
     The tongue of the wise dispenses knowledge,
     but the mouths of fools pour out folly.

4   A gentle tongue is a tree of life,
     but perverseness in it breaks the spirit.

7   The lips of the wise spread knowledge;
     not so the minds of fools.

14   The mind of him who has understanding seeks knowledge,
     but the mouths of fools feed on folly.

26   The thoughts of the wicked are an abomination to the
LORD,
the words of the pure are pleasing to him.

28   The mind of the righteous ponders how to answer,
but the mouth of the wicked pours out evil things.

DAY FOURTEEN

Chapter 16

Lord, speak to me so that I may speak for thee.

1   The plans of the mind belong to man,
but the answer of the tongue is from the LORD.

10   Inspired decisions are on the lips of a king;
his mouth does not sin in judgment.

13   Righteous lips are the delight of a king,
and he loves him who speaks what is right.

DAY FIFTEEN

Chapter 16

Forgive my words, Lord, and help me to forgive others theirs.

23–24 The mind of the wise makes his speech judicious,
and adds persuasiveness to his lips.
Pleasant words are like a honeycomb,
sweetness to the soul and health to the body.

27   A worthless man plots evil,
and his speech is like a scorching fire.

28   A perverse man spreads strife,
      and a whisperer separates close friends.

DAY SIXTEEN

Chapter 17

O Lord, Grant me to hear your "well-done, my friend" today so that I may also say "my friend, well-done."

4   An evildoer listens to wicked lips;
     and a liar gives heed to a mischievous tongue.

7   Fine speech is not becoming to a fool;
     still less is false speech to a prince.

10   A rebuke goes deeper into a man of understanding
     than a hundred blows into a fool.

20   A man of crooked mind does not prosper,
     and one with a perverse tongue falls into calamity.

27–28 He who restrains his words has knowledge,
     and he who has a cool spirit is a man of understanding.
     Even a fool who keeps silent is considered wise;
     when he closes his lips, he is deemed intelligent.

DAY SEVENTEEN

Chapter 18

O Lord, May I mouth thee today and not me.

2   A fool takes no pleasure in understanding,
     but only in expressing his opinion.

4   The words of a man's mouth are deep waters;
       the fountain of wisdom is a gushing stream.

6–8   A fool's lips bring strife,
       and his mouth invites a flogging.
       A fool's mouth is his ruin,
       and his lips are a snare to himself.
       The words of a whisperer are like delicious morsels;
       they go down into the inner parts of the body.

13   If one gives answer before he hears,
       it is his folly and shame.

20–21 From the fruit of his mouth a man is satisfied;
       he is satisfied by the yield of his lips.
       Death and life are in the power of the tongue,
       and those who love it will eat its fruits.

DAY EIGHTEEN

Chapter 19

O Lord, Teach me how best to say I love you; how best to say I love others.

1   Better is a poor man who walks in his integrity
       than a man who is perverse in speech, and is a fool.

5   A false witness will not go unpunished,
       and he who utters lies will not escape.

9   A false witness will not go unpunished,
       and he who utters lies will perish.

16   He who keeps the commandment keeps his life;
      he who despises the word will die.

20   Listen to advice and accept instruction,
      that you may gain wisdom for the future.

27–28 Cease, my son, to hear instruction
      only to stray from the words of knowledge.
      A worthless witness mocks at justice,
      and the mouth of the wicked devours iniquity.

DAY NINETEEN

Chapter 20

O Lord, Let me hear you speak so I can speak what I hear.

15   There is gold, and abundance of costly stones;
      but the lips of knowledge are a precious jewel.

17   Bread gained by deceit is sweet to a man,
      but afterward his breath will be full of gravel.

19–20 He who goes about gossiping reveals secrets;
      therefore do not associate with one who speaks foolishly.
      If one curses his father or his mother,
      his lamp will be put out in utter darkness.

DAY TWENTY

Chapter 21

O Lord, Let soul-song resound from heart and lips today I pray.

6   The getting of treasures by a lying tongue
      is a fleeting vapor and a snare of death.

13   He who closes his ear to the cry of the poor
will himself cry out and not be heard.

23   He who keeps his mouth and his tongue
keeps himself out of trouble.

DAY TWENTY-ONE
Chapter 22

Thou speaking today, may I ever listening be.

10–11 Drive out a scoffer, and strife will go out,
and quarreling and abuse will cease.
He who loves purity of heart, and whose speech is
gracious,
will have the king as his friend.

14   The mouth of a loose woman is a deep pit;
he with whom the Lord is angry will fall into it.

17–18 Incline your ear, and hear the words of the wise,
and apply your mind to my knowledge;
for it will be pleasant if you keep them within you,
if all of them are ready on your lips.

DAY TWENTY-TWO
Chapter 23

O Lord, Help me to learn to speak the phrases of life.

9   Do not speak in the hearing of a fool,
for he will despise the wisdom of your words.

12   Apply your mind to instruction
and your ear to words of knowledge.

16   My soul will rejoice
when your lips speak what is right.

DAY TWENTY-THREE
Chapter 24
Let holy laughter be in my heart and on my mouth.

1–2   Be not envious of evil men,
nor desire to be with them;
for their minds devise violence,
and their lips talk of mischief.

26   He who gives a right answer kisses the lips.

28–29 Be not a witness against your neighbor without cause,
and do not deceive with your lips.
Do not say, "I will do to him as he has done to me;
I will pay the man back for what he has done."

DAY TWENTY-FOUR
Chapter 25
O Lord, Help me to be wise in every word.

11–12 A word fitly spoken is like apples of gold in a setting of
silver.
Like a gold ring or an ornament of gold
is a wise reprover to a listening ear.

15   With patience a ruler may be persuaded,
and a soft tongue will break a bone.

18   A man who bears false witness against his neighbor
is like a war club, or a sword, or a sharp arrow.

23   The north wind brings forth rain;
      and a backbiting tongue, angry looks.

27   It is not good to eat much honey,
      so be sparing of complimentary words.

DAY TWENTY-FIVE
Chapter 26

O Lord, Forgive my critical tongue; teach it compassion and the rich habit of affirmation.

2   Like a sparrow in its flitting, like a swallow in its flying,
      a curse that is causeless does not alight.

4–5   Answer not a fool according to his folly,
      lest you be like him yourself.
      Answer a fool according to his folly,
      lest he be wise in his own eyes.

7   Like a lame man's legs, which hang useless,
      is a proverb in the mouth of fools.

9   Like a thorn that goes up into the hand of a drunkard
      is a proverb in the mouth of fools.

17   He who meddles in a quarrel not his own
      is like one who takes a passing dog by the ears.

DAY TWENTY-SIX
Chapter 26

O Lord, Help me to learn not to whisper what I would never speak out loud.

20-23 For lack of wood the fire goes out;
and where there is no whisperer, quarreling ceases.
As charcoal to hot embers and wood to fire,
so is a quarrelsome man for kindling strife.
The words of a whisperer are like delicious morsels;
they go down into the inner parts of the body.
Like the glaze covering an earthen vessel
are smooth lips with an evil heart.

24-26 He who hates, dissembles with his lips
and harbors deceit in his heart;
when he speaks graciously, believe him not,
for there are seven abominations in his heart;
though his hatred be covered with guile,
his wickedness will be exposed in the assembly.

28　　A lying tongue hates its victims,
and a flattering mouth works ruin.

DAY TWENTY-SEVEN
Chapter 27

O Lord, Help me to hear what people say and to say what they need to hear.

2　　Let another praise you, and not your own mouth;
a stranger, and not your own lips.

5　　Better is open rebuke than hidden love.

14　　He who blesses his neighbor with a loud voice,
rising early in the morning, will be counted as cursing.

DAY TWENTY-EIGHT

Chapter 28

Let my tongue give no offense today, Father.

13   He who conceals his transgressions will not prosper,
but he who confesses and forsakes them will obtain
mercy.

23   He who rebukes a man will afterward find more favor
than he who flatters with his tongue.

TWENTY-NINE

Chapter 29

Today, in every way, may I bless the Lord.

18–19 Where there is no prophecy the people cast off restraint,
but blessed is he who keeps the law.
By mere words a servant is not disciplined,
for though he understands, he will not give heed.

20   Do you see a man who is hasty in his words?
There is more hope for a fool than for him.

DAY THIRTY

Chapter 30

O Lord, May the welcome I give today be from my heart.

5–6   Every word of God proves true;
he is a shield to those who take refuge in him.
Do not add to his words, lest he rebuke you,
and you be found a liar.

8–9   Remove far from me falsehood and lying;
       give me neither poverty or riches;
       feed me with the food that is needful for me,
       lest I be full, and deny thee, and say, "Who is the Lord?"
       or lest I be poor, and steal, and profane the name of my God.

DAY THIRTY-ONE
Chapter 31

O Lord, Empty the old treasures of my heart today so I may fill it with the new treasure of yourself.

26   She opens her mouth with wisdom,
       and the teaching of kindness is on her tongue.

THE EVENING PRAYER

My Lord,
As one more day closes,
Reveal
If my mouth has brought unnecessary pain,
If I have spoken death
If my tongue has been a device of torture
If I have sinned by speaking,
By keeping silent.

Forgive me, I pray.
I am truly sorry and do most humbly repent.
Give me again, tomorrow,
The gift of life.
Help me to speak it into the lives of others.
Amen.